Quick and Fun Games for Babies

Katie Eyles, M. Ed.

Teacher Created Materials, Inc.

Cover Design by Chris Macabitas

Illustrated by Blanca Apodaca

www.teachercreated.com

Made in U.S.A.

ISBN 1-57690-358-3

Order Number TCM 2358

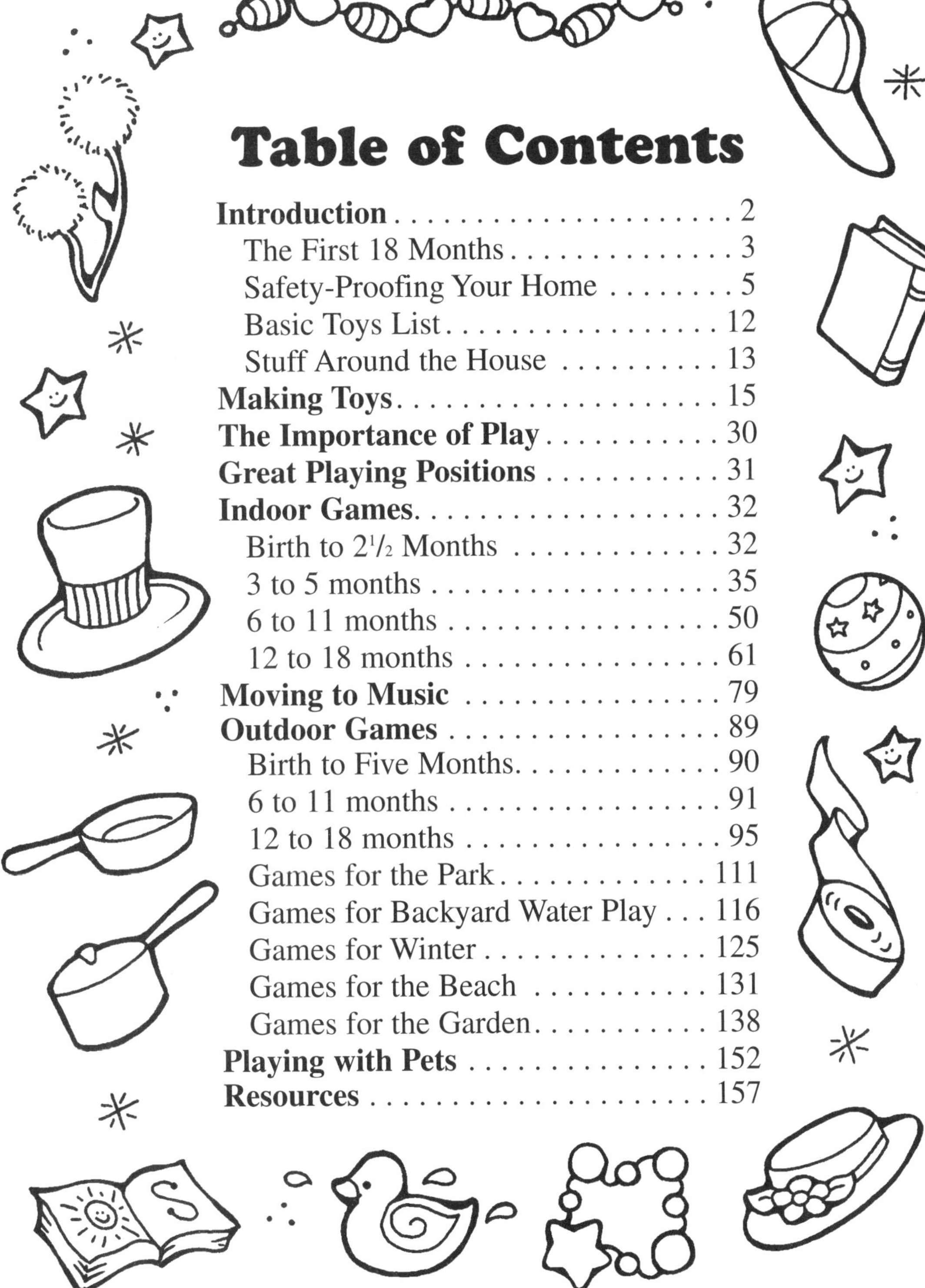

Table of Contents

Introduction

When they are sleeping, babies are rosy-cheeked cherubs, little miracles with tiny fingers and toes. When they are awake, they transform into world explorers. Curiosity leads them into new lands: drawers, closets, cabinets, and underneath furniture. Everything is brand new, and everything is exciting.

Through their enthusiasm, we, as parents and teachers, are allowed to experience the world anew. No longer is a bath just a way to keep clean. It becomes an opportunity for exploration and fun. A mundane trip to the grocery store is now an adventure in socialization and an opportunity to discover new textures, colors, and sounds. No longer is a walk across the yard a routine event. Babies are fascinated by a blade of grass and blowing dandelions. They believe trees are giants and lightning bugs are magic.

During these times of exploration and play, babies are learning about their world's colors, shapes, textures, and sounds. They are also learning about themselves: how to move, how to make sounds, how to respond to others, and much more. In the first 18 months of life, babies learn quickly and naturally. We, as the parents and teachers of our children, are their facilitators and cheerleaders. We help provide opportunities in which learning occurs naturally, and we provide the encouragement our babies need to accomplish their developmental goals. We also make sure that our babies are safe while they are learning.

In this book there are more than a hundred activities to provide busy parents with inexpensive and interesting opportunities to promote learning while having fun with their babies. The book is divided into two large sections: Indoor Games and Outdoor Games. Each section lists activities by the ages children typically develop the skills needed to participate. Included in this book are ideas for safety-proofing your home, room by room, and for making toys with items you have around the house. At the end of the book, you will find great Internet sites for parents, resources, and recommended books. This book is designed as a quick and easy reference so that you have even more time to play with your baby!

The First 18 Months

During the first 18 months, babies are constantly changing, both physically and mentally. When babies first come home from the hospital, they spend most of their time sleeping. When they are awake, they may be irritable because they are wet and/or hungry. This stage usually lasts about six weeks. During that time, you are primarily a comforter. You try to make baby as comfortable as possible in her new environment.

After the first six weeks, baby begins to be more aware of her environment. She is beginning to discover her hands. They are an endless source of fascination for her. She also has more control of her body, lifting her head and moving her arms and legs more. But most importantly, she is beginning to discover you, your voice, and especially your face. This is also the age when that ever important smile emerges! Your role is now growing from simply a comforter to a comforter and facilitator. During this time of discovery, you are supplying her with opportunities to begin her exploration.

By three-and-one-half to five months, your baby will be delighting in her newfound skills. She will enjoy kicking her feet, rolling over, and lifting her head to survey the new world around her. She may also be enjoying hearing herself babble. She will want to explore everything in detail, using her eyes, ears, hands, and mouth. In this stage, you are supporting her exploration as well as creating a special bond with her.

From five-and-one-half to eight months, she is a busy girl indeed. No more of this lying around the house for her! She reaches for objects, turns over, sits up, and may even start crawling. Dropping and throwing objects are also sources of discovery and entertainment. Words begin to take on meaning for her. The words "bottle" and "mommy" really may mean something to her now. In this phase, not only do you continue to do all the things you did before, but now you have to really be concerned about keeping her safe. She is beginning to move around, and she knows no danger.

From eight months to fourteen months, a whole new world opens up to your baby. She begins to stand, pull up, and cruise furniture, and then comes the moment you've been waiting for—she takes her first step! Before those first steps, she may have started saying a few words. Don't become alarmed if she doesn't say many new words or stops saying most words completely.

The First 18 Months *(cont.)*

She is having to concentrate on these new motor skills. Once walking becomes easier for her, she will probably begin talking again. Remember, language expression typically begins somewhere between eight and twenty months. While baby is learning all of these advanced skills, she will actually start requesting help from you, if not with words, then with gestures and sounds. She will love being around you, although she may not be too happy about being around strangers. (You may have to remind Aunt Millie not to be offended by baby's shyness. It is just a natural phase she is entering.) Since baby is now walking, your role as a monitor for her safety becomes absolutely crucial, especially if she is extremely active. Remember, baby still does not understand danger. Along with being a safety monitor, your role as disciplinarian starts emerging. As you begin to redirect your child, you are establishing patterns that will make the more challenging years much easier!

As your baby enters the stage between 15 to 18 months, she becomes a world explorer. She not only enjoys roaming around the house, but she loves outside time. Every once in awhile, she may take a break from her explorations to watch TV or videos or listen to a story, but probably not for long! She may start taking some interest in other children, but her primary interest is still you. Enjoy it while it lasts because after the age of two, she will become more and more independent and more and more involved with her peers. In this phase, she may be perfecting those motor skills acquired in the last phase, but she will also be adding a few new ones, including climbing up and down stairs. By 18 months, she may even be walking up and down steps while holding your hand. Running and jumping skills are also likely to emerge. Finally, language development is very important during this time. Baby already understands a lot, and now she will usually begin saying a lot of single words and even perhaps begin experimenting with putting two words together. So you see, birth to 18 months is an incredible time filled with changes for both you and your baby.

Food Safety

Your Child's Food

Believe it not, some foods can actually be a hazard to your young child. Choking, unhealthy bacteria, and food allergies are all food-related problems that may affect your child's health. Here are a few hints about ways to help keep your child safe.

Choking

Four thousand people in the United States die each year from choking. Children under the age of four are at the greatest risk. When they are just beginning to eat table food, babies often choke. Some of the most dangerous foods for this age group include hot dogs, nuts, hard candy, grapes, popcorn, apples with peel, raw carrots, raisins, and other hard, round foods that can block a baby's air passage.

Bacteria

Guard against unhealthy bacteria by keeping hot foods hot and cold foods cold. Make sure meats and eggs are well cooked. Wash vegetables and fruits and always wash your hands before and after handling food.

Food Allergies

As strange as it seems, some children are allergic to milk. Other common food allergies for young children include eggs, peanuts, any tree nuts (example: walnuts), fish, shellfish, soy, and wheat.

If your baby is experiencing hives, wheezing, vomiting, redness of skin, diarrhea, or swelling of lips, mouth, or throat shortly after feeding, check with your doctor about the possibility of a food allergy. If your child is eating table food, all you have to do is avoid the food. If your child is on formula, don't panic! Today, many different formulas exist. One will be right for your baby.

Poisonous Plants

Many of the plants around your house and yard can be hazardous to your young child. Here is a list of plants that are considered dangerous if swallowed.

- Aloe
- Amaryllis
- Azalea
- Bird-of-Paradise
- Candelabra Cactus
- Carolina Jessamine
- Castor Bean
- Chinaberry Tree
- Cotoneaster
- Cyclamen
- Daffodil
- Dumb Cane
- Eucalyptus
- Evening Trumpet Flower
- Foxglove
- Holly
- Indian Tobacco
- Iris
- Jimson Weed
- Lantana

Poisonous Plants *(cont.)*

- Mistletoe
- Mole Bean
- Morning Glory
- Oleander
- Poppy
- Periwinkle
- Philodendron
- Poison Ivy
- Potato
- Pothos
- Primula
- Privet
- Rhododendron
- Rosebay
- Silverleaf Nightshade
- Texas Mountain Laurel
- Tree Tobacco
- Water Hemlock
- Yellow Oleander

Safety-Proofing

Your Family Room

Since much of your time as a family is spent in this room, you need to make sure it is a safe environment for your child. Read the suggestions below.

1. Remove plants that baby can reach; some may be poisonous, and others may just make a mess if tipped over.
2. Put non-skid tape under rugs.
3. Secure heavy, unbalanced furniture.
4. Put padding on furniture with sharp corners.
5. Put decals on sliding glass doors.
6. Remove items that baby can break or swallow.
7. Put electrical cords behind furniture or use a cord shortener.
8. Tie up window-blind cords.
9. Place safety gates in front of all stairs.
10. Lock up guns and ammunition.
11. Cover all unused electrical outlets.

Safety-Proofing *(cont.)*

Your Kitchen

The kitchen can be one of the most hazardous places in the house for your young child. Look at the diagram below to see some of the precautions you can take and read the suggestions for safety-proofing.

1. Try to use back burners. If you can't, always remember to turn handles inward so baby can't grab them.
2. Install a stove lock or guard.
3. Lock away dangerous chemicals, pet foods, and cat litter.
4. Keep a fire extinguisher handy. It should also be out of baby's reach.
5. Keep knives and other sharp utensils out of baby's reach.
6. Put a lock on the trash can and any cabinets containing unsafe items.
7. Remove tablecloths and hanging items your baby might grab onto or pull down.
8. Cover all unused wall sockets.

Safety-Proofing *(cont.)*

Your Laundry Room

Not every home has a laundry room, but most homes have a washer and dryer. These appliances have long been children's favorite hiding places, resulting in serious injuries. Look at the diagram below and safety-proof the space that is considered your laundry room.

1. Lock dryers and washers, if possible. If not, you may want to lock the laundry room.
2. Keep detergents, cleaning supplies, and chemicals in a high cupboard or under lock and key.
3. Unplug the iron after use and store.
4. Cover all plugs not being used.
5. Some laundry rooms have extra refrigerators or freezers. You may consider locking them as well. They are dangerous "hiding places."
6. Make sure there are no dangling cords from windows or outlets.

Safety-Proofing *(cont.)*

Your Bathroom

Next to the kitchen, the bathroom may be the most hazardous room in your home for a small child. Look at the diagram and read the suggestions below for safety-proofing your bathroom.

1. Never leave your child alone in the bathroom.
2. Lock away all chemicals and medicines.
3. Keep electrical appliances away from water areas and out of baby's reach.
4. Always test the water before putting your child in the tub.
5. Install a lock on the toilet.
6 Use a faucet cover in the tub when bathing a child.
7. Adjust your water heater to a lower temperature to decrease the chance of your child being severely burned.
8. Use skid-proof mats on floors and put skid-proof stickers on tub bottoms.

Basic Toys List

If you prefer to buy your toys rather than make them, or you'd like to have some of both, here is a simple list for 1 to 18 month olds.

- Activity blankets
- Activity centers
- Books
- Blocks
- Dish set for babies
- Mobiles
- Plastic bucket and shovel
- Rattles
- Recorded music for babies
- Safety mirrors to attach to cribs
- Soft, small balls (not too small)
- Toys that light up and make noises when baby pushes a button
- Stuffed animals and dolls (Be careful about removable small parts.)
- Trucks, cars, and other push toys

Stuff Around the House

Many expensive toys for very young children are on the market today. However, you may have items around your house that your young child will like just as well. Often, you don't even need toys to play with your baby. Stimulation from you is how your child learns at this stage. He is watching the way you move your lips to make sounds, listening to the sounds you are making to form words, discovering new textures by feeling your hair or your skin, and socializing by watching the way you smile at him and then smiling back at you. Your contact with him at this age is much more important than the toys you use in play.

When you do decide to include toys in your play, here is a list of some basic materials you may already have around your house that he may like. You may want to collect the materials you have and throw them into a box so that they will be easy to find. Start collecting and use your imagination. What else might be fun to include?

Some of the materials listed below will be used in the Making Toys section of this book. You can use these materials in many of the activities that follow. However, feel free to make up new games and new activities. As your child grows, you may be surprised at the number of new activities he creates with these common household items. Remember though to keep safety as your first priority.

- Books with large, colorful pictures
- Baby wipes boxes
- Boxes of different sizes
- Clean, old panty hose
- Construction paper and poster board
- Egg cartons
- Family photo albums
- Hats and caps

Stuff Around the House *(cont.)*

- Holiday tree lights*
- Index cards
- Large pieces of fabric, old tablecloths
- Lightweight pots and pans with lids
- Magazines with big pictures of people, animals, and objects
- Necklaces and bracelets
- Plastic containers, milk bottles, and cups
- Ribbon and string
- Round containers (oatmeal, raisins)
- Safety mirrors
- Scrapbooks
- Socks that no longer have matches
- Tape recorder, CD player, radio, tapes, and CDs
- Video tape recorder, videotapes
- Wrapping paper tubes
- Wooden spoons

**Use only lights that have been tested for safety by a recognized testing laboratory. Regularly check each set of lights for broken sockets and frayed wires before using them. Never leave them on when you go to bed or leave the house. Of course, you should never leave your young child unsupervised with these lights.*

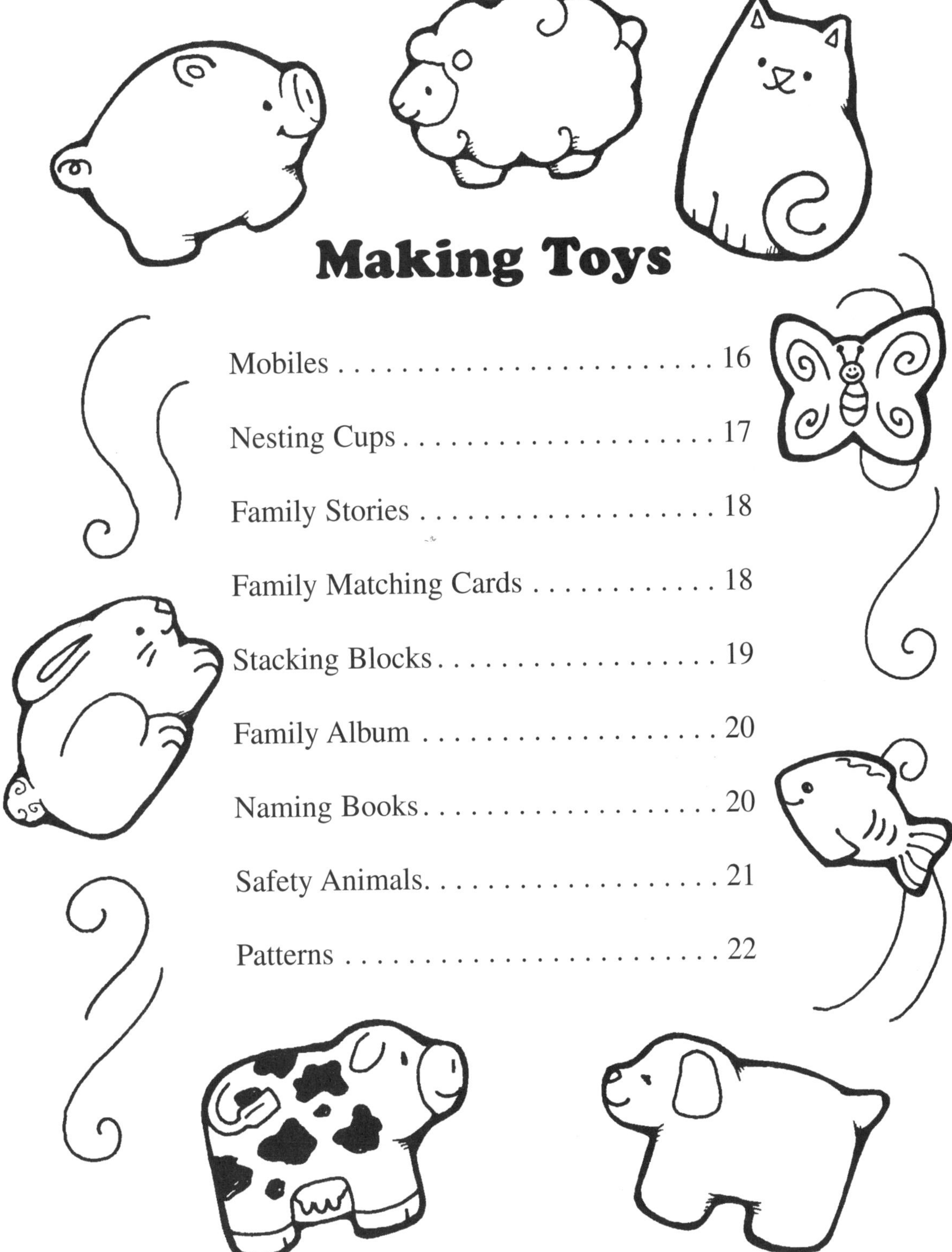

Making Toys

Mobiles

Materials

- Construction paper
- Felt pens
- Magazine pictures
- Pictures
- Poster board
- Scissors
- String

Store-bought mobiles are pretty, but they may not be as effective as ones you make yourself. You also may like the idea of changing mobiles as your child develops. To sidestep the additional cost of all the changes, try a few of these ideas.

Your baby's first mobile should be black and white and should probably be a face. The black and white provides contrast, which attracts the baby's attention better than pastels or muted colors. The face, especially between the tip of the nose and the top of the head, is an area that appears naturally interesting to babies. Cut an oblong shape out of poster board. Color some black hair on the figure, put two solid black eyes, two black eyebrows, a black line for a nose, and one for the mouth on it. Hang the mobile a few inches from your baby's face. Young babies can focus but do not see clearly, so they will lose interest in an object that is any farther than 18 inches from their eyes.

Your second mobile may be black, white, and red lines in any shape. You may want to cut out a circle, triangle, and square. Make each piece look like a maze of black and red lines on white paper. You will be surprised how these designs get your baby's attention. Move the mobile farther away out of baby's reach since she is more physically active now.

You may want your baby's third mobile to be of her favorite characters. Make it easy on yourself and color pictures from a coloring book or use laminated magazine pictures.

Nesting Cups

Materials

- Contact paper
- Different-sized plastic containers
- Different-sized plastic glasses
- Different-sized cans
- Measuring cups

If you are looking for a place to save a few dollars, don't bother buying nesting cups. You probably have a variety of items around the house that will do exactly the same thing. The concept behind nesting cups is to get baby to realize the differences in sizes and to understand that smaller containers can go into larger containers. In other words, you are laying the groundwork for some basic math skills later in your baby's development.

If you have several plastic containers around the house, see if you have three that will fit neatly inside each other. If you do, you have your first set of nesting cups.

Another option helps the earth as well as your baby: Take different-sized cans that you were going to throw out, wash them, file around the top to make sure rough edges are gone, and put contact paper over the cans to make them colorful and safer.

If you still haven't found the perfect nesting cups for your baby, or you just want a little variety, sort through your plastic glasses to see if you have different sizes that will fit in each other.

When he gets into your pots and pans one of his activities will probably include putting the small pans inside the bigger ones.

Family Stories

Materials

- Action shots of family
- Markers
- Scissors
- Scrapbook
- Stickers

Make a scrapbook of family stories. You may want the first story to be about a day in the life of your family. You can talk to baby about family routines. Include action shots of the family doing things together. Put it in an accessible place so that you can easily share it with your baby. If you have older children, you may want them to write some of the stories or to take some of the pictures. You will probably have as much fun reading the book and looking at the pictures as your baby does.

Family Matching Cards

Materials

- Cardboard frames or mat frames
- Duplicate head shots of family members

Make two cards for each family member. Place pictures in attractive cardboard frames. You now have a complete set of matching cards that can be used for a variety of games. You can use them as flashcards. You can lay one picture of each person's face on a table or on the floor. Let baby point to the pictures as you name the names. Finally, for a more advanced game, turn the cards facedown. Take turns selecting cards and trying to find a match for each card.

Stacking Blocks

Materials

- Baby wipes boxes
- Cereal boxes
- Coffee containers
- Oatmeal boxes

If you don't want to spend money on stacking blocks, you really don't have to. You can use any of the boxes listed and not only help your pocketbook but also help the Earth. Instead of throwing away, you are recycling. Just tape the ends. You can cover them with paper or contact paper if you would like, but baby will probably like them just as they are.

Family Album

Materials

- Album
- Recent family pictures

A family album should be a special book for you and baby. Shop around until you find an album you really like. Select very clear, recent pictures of your family members. Black and white pictures are sometimes even better than color. Place the pictures in the album and keep it an easily accessible place so it won't be hard to find anytime you want to take a few minutes to flip through the pages and tell baby about family members.

Naming Books

Materials

- Drawings
- Old magazines
- Pictures

Been looking for a use for all those old magazines? Cut out pictures as you watch TV and paste them into a book. You will have a ready reference for your baby. You may want to make several types of books: an animal book, people book, object book, etc.

Safety Animals

Materials

- Needle
- Thread
- Scissors
- Patterns
- 100% polyester, non-allergenic stuffing

Afraid of eyes or noses that come off store-bought animals? Cut out the patterns on the following pages. Cut material to fit the patterns. Make the eyes, noses, and mouths out of embroidery stitches. Sew all but one side of the animals together. Stuff them. Sew the last side closed. Now you have animals your young baby can play with, and you don't have to worry about parts coming off.

***Note:** (Polyester stuffing is easily washable, and non-allergenic stuffing is an important safeguard against possible fabric allergies your baby may have.)*

Dog Pattern

Cat Pattern

Butterfly Pattern

Cow Pattern

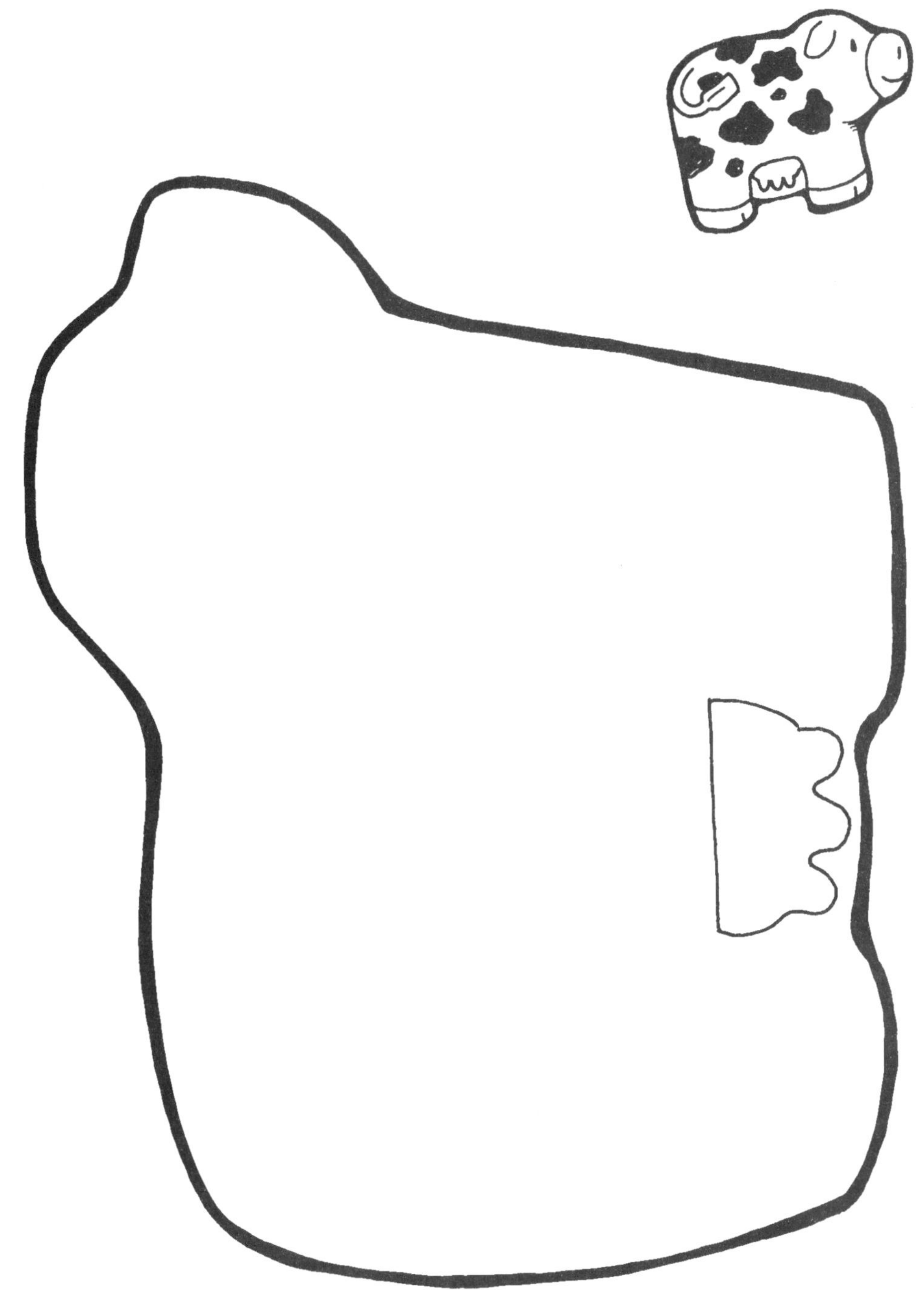

Bunny Pattern

Pig Pattern

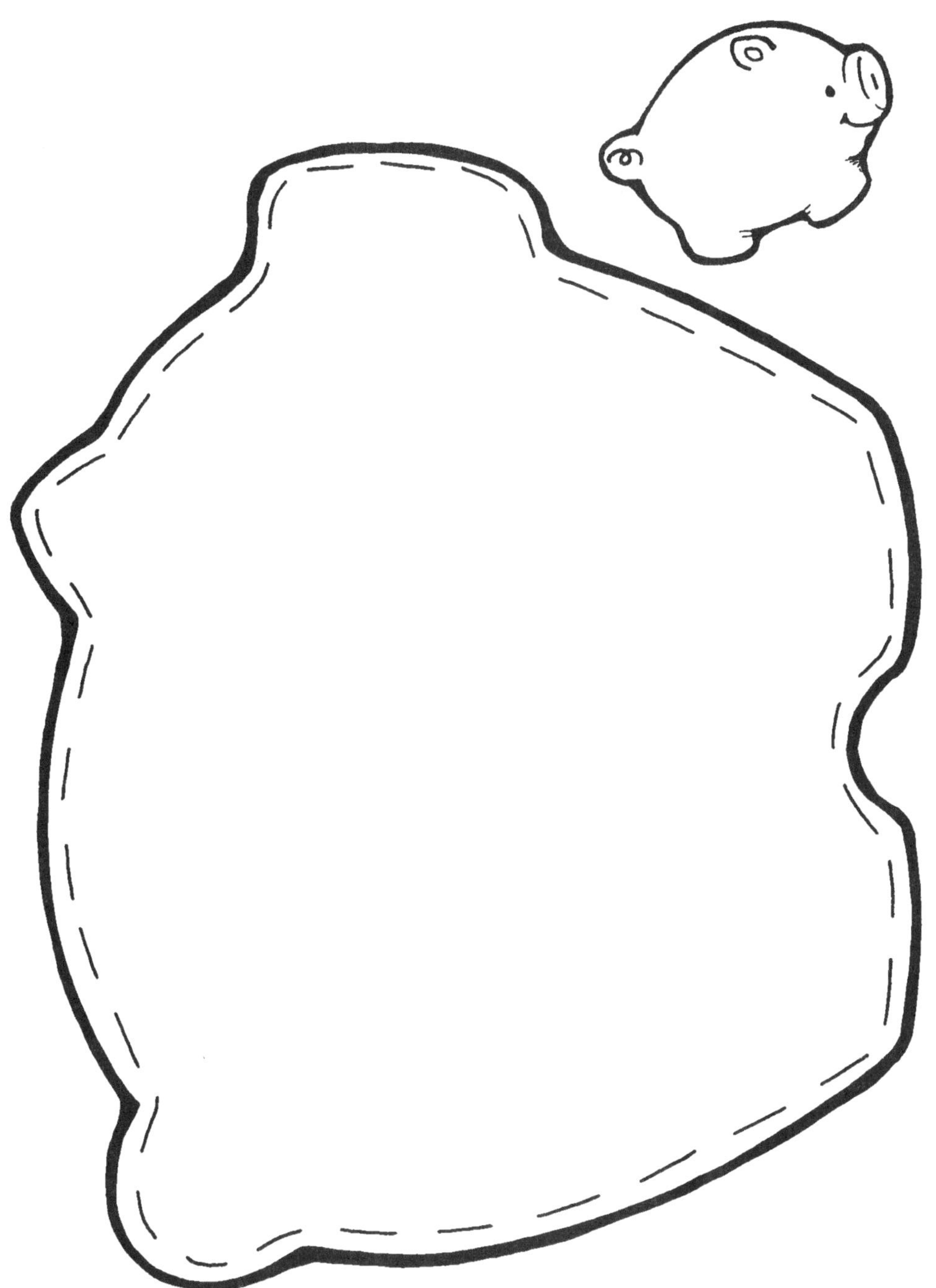

Lamb Pattern

Fish Pattern

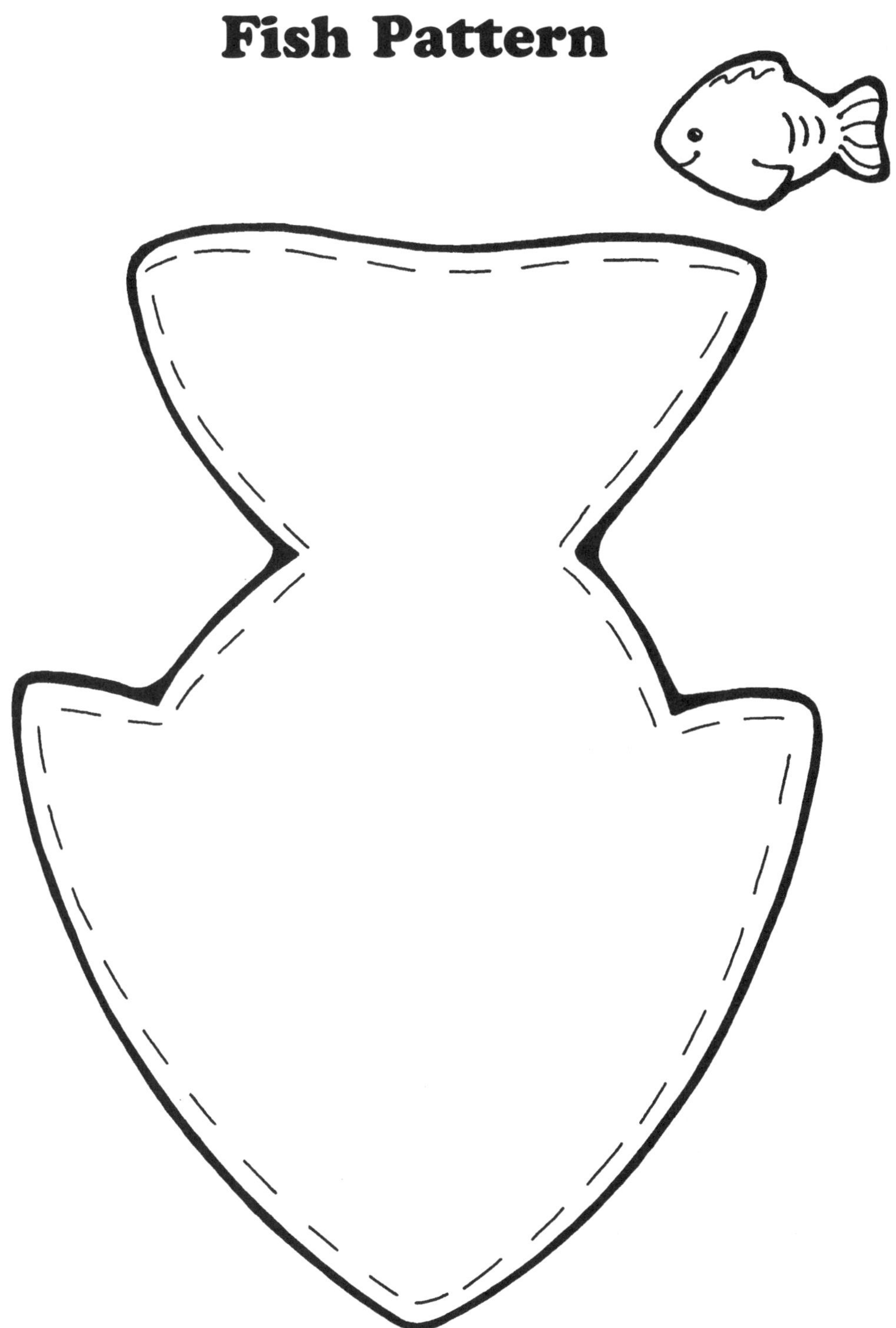

The Importance of Play

Never feel guilty about playing with your child. Believe it or not, he is learning and you are teaching him through play. During the first few weeks of life, baby spends most of his time sleeping. He is adjusting to his new world. He hasn't learned to play yet, but he is enjoying all the comforts and security you are providing him. Some of his favorite activities are eating, sleeping and being gently rocked by you.

By week six though, he is beginning to enjoy games. He has found his hands and enjoys watching what they will do. During this time, simple grasping games are very effective. While you are having fun, remember that you are also helping him develop the small muscles in his hands that control his fine motor skills.

At three months, your baby is really enjoying play. He is developing rapidly and acquiring all types of new skills. Games that help him develop those large muscles in his body are especially exciting to him. He seems to enjoy reaching and trying to roll over. He has also become quite the social creature. He enjoys playing with you. Games give you a chance to spend time bonding with him. Your relationship with him is extremely important because you are helping him form social patterns he will use for the rest of his life.

The time between eight and eighteen months is packed with new skill development. Your baby is beginning to explore the world from different perspectives. No longer is he on his back or tummy only. He can crawl, sit up, stand, walk, and even run. The world is a fascinating place to him and he loves new games that keep him moving and introduce him to new concepts. Along with his large and small muscle skill development, his language is also rapidly developing. By playing games with him that emphasize simple vocabulary and sentence structure, you are teaching him new words and basic language patterns. Finally, his social skills are continuing to develop primarily through his interactions with you. Games you play with him now lay the foundation for important social skills that he will need later, such as following directions and sharing.

Games are important teaching tools. They are effective because they are an enjoyable way for you to teach your baby, and a natural way for your baby to learn.

Great Playing Positions

When you are playing with your baby, there are four positions you may want to use. They may give her more freedom of movement and allow her a better line of vision.

Instead of putting your newborn to two-and-a-half-month-old baby on her back and under her gym, try placing her in a carrier and putting her gym in front of her. She can see better, and she doesn't have to work against gravity to move.

Instead of carrying baby with her face over your shoulder, try carrying her facing forward in a supported, sitting position. Her hands and feet will have more freedom, and she can see much better.

Even at a very young age, place baby on her tummy for short periods of time. This will encourage her to lift her head up to explore, and she will be able to see better.

When your baby is learning how to sit but is unable to sit alone, you should sit down, separate your legs, and put baby in front of you. You will be surprised how long she will stay in that position with your support. You are giving her more freedom of movement and a better line of vision when playing.

Indoor Games Birth to 2½ Months

Bedtime Mirror

Materials

- Safety mirror

Very young babies spend most of their time sleeping. However, even at a very young age, babies do seem to be interested in mirrors. Attach a safety mirror to the inside of the crib and close to baby's head. When she wakes up, she will have something amusing to watch.

Face Mobile

Materials

- Face Mobile (See Making Toys, page, 16.)

Now is the time for the face mobile. Babies become interested in looking at faces when they are around six weeks of age. Their vision still isn't well developed. The simple pattern and contrast of the black and white makes the mobile easy for baby to see.

Rocking the Night Away

Game

Materials

- Rocker
- Soothing music or sounds

Sometimes newborns are difficult to comfort. They may have gas or colic and cry. The oldest method of soothing a grumpy baby is rocking. Try adding sounds of running water or soft classical music to attempt to soothe your baby.

Swinging

Game

Materials

- Battery-operated swing

Whenever you get nostalgic about the good old days, just remember battery-operated swings did not exist. You don't want to leave your baby in these swings for long periods of time, but they do provide a little relief for tired or busy moms. Just put baby in the swing, turn it on, and let the swing rock baby for a few minutes. You can take a minute to relax and watch your baby. This activity is guaranteed to leave both of your blissfully content. Never leave your baby unattended in the swing, however.

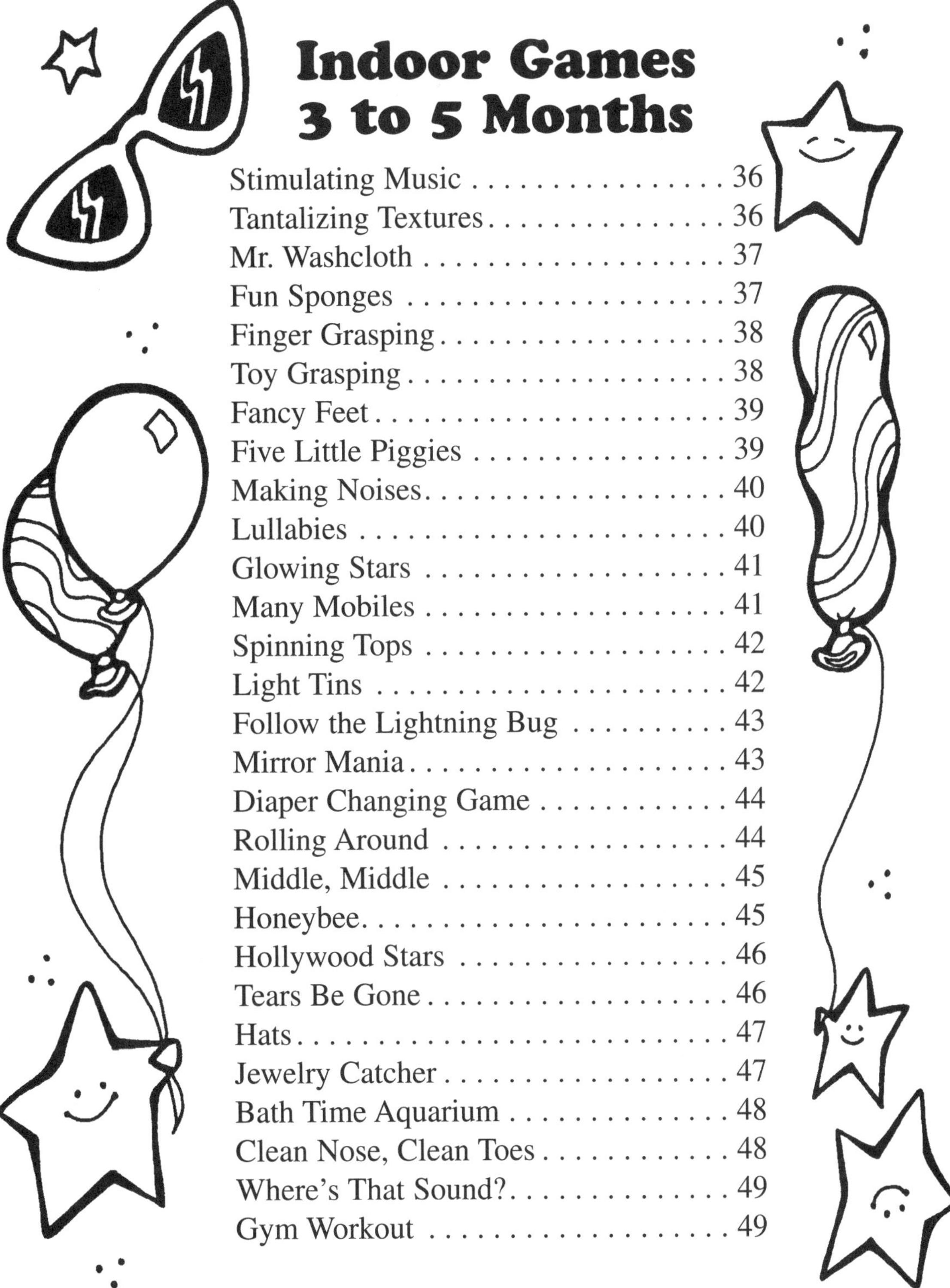

Indoor Games 3 to 5 Months

Stimulating Music

Materials

- CD, Tape Player, or Radio
- Classical Music

Game

A very simple and pleasant game to play with your newborn is the Stimulating Music game. Take a blanket big enough for two and put it on the floor near the stereo. Pop in a disc of classical music and watch your baby's reactions. If you don't have a stereo, grab your radio and turn it to your local classical station. Usually, classical stations play a variety of music, and it is all free! Soon you will discover which tunes make him laugh, smile, and sometimes even go to sleep. Don't be surprised if your playmate drifts off to dreamland before the end of the game.

Tantalizing Textures

Materials

- Cardboard box
- Textured materials

Game

Newborns are exploring a brand new world, and different textures fascinate them. Collect a variety of textured materials from around the house. Keep in mind that the items should not have sharp points or have small pieces that can be easily swallowed. Sit with your baby on a blanket on the floor. Play with her using various textured items from the box. Take a soft texture, like a silk scarf, and rub it on her cheek or take a fuzzy texture, like a stuffed animal, and rub it on her tummy. As your newborn develops, she will still enjoy playing the game. Just be sure that objects can be put safely in an infant's mouth since young babies like to use their mouths to explore.

Mr. Washcloth

Materials

- Washcloth
- Tub
- Water

Game

Even very young babies can benefit from water play. Mr. Washcloth is a fun, but simple game. Take your index finger and insert it in the middle of the washcloth. Let the rest of your cloth fall around your finger so that it looks like a ghost. Move your finger up and down and say things like, "Mr. Washcloth is here to see you. He wants to kiss your tummy." Move your finger to your baby's tummy and make a kissing sound. Then while you're there, wash the baby's tummy. Your baby will smile and laugh while you clean. A bonus to this game is that baby will begin hearing the names of body parts.

Fun Sponges

Materials

- Various sponges
- Tub
- Water

Game

Sponges come in all sizes, shapes, and colors. Some of the sponges that are the most fun to use when playing with babies and young children are the pop-up sponges. Put your baby in a sitting position. Show him the flat sponge. Put it in the water in front of him and watch him smile as the flat sponge pops up. Sponges that come in the shapes of animals are especially popular with young children. Use the sponge to bathe your baby or let your child play with the sponge while you clean your baby.

Finger Grasping

Game

Materials

- None

One of the first games your child will participate in is finger grasping. Place her on the floor on a blanket. Take your index finger and pass it slowly in front of your baby's face. She will probably visually try to follow your finger. As your baby develops, the distance she tracks your finger should increase. Move your finger to her hand. Allow her to grasp your finger in all five little fingers. Talk to her and smile at her as she grasps your fingers. You have just made one of her first attempts at socialization a positive experience.

Toy Grasping

Game

Materials

- Stuffed animal

Soon your child will outgrow your finger and want to move on to grasping toys. Rattles are wonderful, but if you want a little variety, select a character that your child enjoys. How about a favorite, brightly-colored stuffed animal? One with big, floppy ears would be easy to grasp. Whatever animal you choose, make sure that there are no small parts that could be easily swallowed. You may want to try using one of the easy-to-make Safety Animals (page 21). Show your child the animal. You may even sing a little song and move the animal around as if it is dancing. Finally, place the animal within reach of your child and encourage him to reach and grasp. Keeping this toy on your diapering table is a good idea to occupy baby during diaper changing. If you want to create added interest, sew bells into the stuffing.

Fancy Feet

Materials

- Fancy socks

Game

It is easy to get your baby to notice his feet during this game. Just put a pair of fancy socks on his feet. These fancy socks are usually bright with contrasting colors. Often, bells are attached to the toes to get the attention of your little one. After you place the socks on his feet, put his feet in your hands and gently pat them together. Naturally, he looks to see what you are doing. As he develops and starts moving his feet, he will be curious when he hears the bells ring and try to pull his feet up so that he can see what's making all the noise. Watch baby at all times to make sure the bells don't get pulled off. Whether you are participating in the game or simply watching him, you will be fascinated by all his antics.

Five Little Piggies

Materials

- None

Game

Five Little Piggies is a game your mother and father may have played with you. It is an old game, but it is still one that makes children laugh. You need to position your baby on his back or in a sitting position. Start wiggling the big toe and say, "This little piggy went to market." Go to the next toe and say, "This little piggy stayed home." When you wiggle the third toe say, "This little piggy ate roast beef." Move to the fourth toe and say, "But this little piggy had none." Wiggle the fifth toe very quickly and say, "This little piggy cried, 'Wee, wee, wee, all the way home." This game is guaranteed to make your baby laugh.

Making Noises

Materials

- None

Game

Imitating your baby's noises may make you feel silly, but you are helping your child with her language development. The best position for this game is for the baby to be on her back or supported in a carrier. Look at your baby and wait for her to make noises. Repeat the noises she makes. You will probably notice that the number of noises she makes will increase. As your baby develops, add different sounds. She will begin imitating the sounds that you make. As she masters one sound, move to the next.

Lullabies

Materials

- Lullabies
- Tape player
- Tape

Game

When you sing a lullaby, you may think that all you are doing is calming your baby before bedtime. Anytime you sing to your baby, you are also helping him develop language. Don't worry if you can't sing well; your baby won't complain. So get a big comfortable rocker, cuddle with your baby, and sing softly to her. You may even keep a tape player by the rocker to provide a soft musical background.

Glowing Stars

Materials

- Glowing adhesive stars

Game

Change your baby's ceiling into an evening sky. Buy a pack of adhesive stars and stick them on your ceiling, or if you want to be even more original, buy star stencils with different colored fluorescent paints. When you put him to bed at night, turn off the lights, hold him, and talk to him about the glowing stars. It is guaranteed to be a pleasant end to both your days.

Many Mobiles

Materials

- Mobiles

Game

When your newborn comes home, he will probably be able to see patterns in white, black, and red better than other colors. As he grows older, bright colors will be more interesting to him. Therefore, instead of having just one mobile above his crib, you may want to change the mobile as your baby's interests change. Initially, with each new mobile, stand at the crib and blow on it to make it move. This will draw your baby's attention to the new toy. Watch your baby's reactions as he watches it slow down, speed up, and change directions. Be careful to secure the mobiles, and remember that mobiles directly over baby's head will not only be difficult to see but may be dangerous if they accidentally come loose or are within the grasp of curious hands.

Spinning Tops

Materials

- Spinning tops

Game

Even very young babies love to watch spinning tops, especially the kind that light up as they spin. Put your baby on her tummy or on her side. Crank up the top and watch your baby smile and laugh as she watches the top. To make this activity a game, wait to crank up the top until she signals you that she wants more. She may wave her hands, kick her feet, or make noises. When she signals you, start the top again. You two are learning to communicate with each other while you're having fun!

Light Tins

Materials

- Black marker
- Different-colored light bulbs
- Ice pick or nail and hammer
- Light
- Small piece of tin (available at craft stores)

Game

Want to give your baby something new to look at while you change her diaper? Take a small piece of tin. At craft stores, you can buy pieces that are light and easy to puncture. Draw a simple shape (circle, triangle, square) or a common animal (dog, cat, sheep, etc.) on the back of the piece of tin with a felt pen. Punch holes about every ¼" (.6 cm) around the outline of the character. (You don't have to be exact.) Take a small light and replace the bulb with a colored light bulb. Prop the tin up in front of the light (a small easel can also be used). Position the light tin in a place your baby can see but not touch it. Since light bulbs and tin are inexpensive, you can change shapes and colors often. While you change her diaper, talk to her about what she sees.

Follow the Lightning Bug

Materials

- Keychain flashlight

Game

Tracking is one of your baby's developmental milestones. Tracking involves your infant being able to watch an object as it moves from right to left, left to right, up and down, down and up, and around. Some babies will track by just looking at your finger or a toy. If your baby has difficulty tracking or you want a little something different to make tracking more fun, take your tiny flashlight off your key chain. Put your baby on the bed, sofa, or on a blanket on the floor on his back. Say, "Here is the little lightning bug. Watch it fly!" Move your flashlight from right to left and left to right. Then move it up and down and all around. Don't expect your infant to be able to follow all the movements. It may take him a couple of months to be able to follow the flashlight in all directions.

Mirror Mania

Materials

- Mirrors

Game

Babies love mirrors! When they are infants, safety mirrors may be attached to their cribs and playpens to provide added visual stimulation. When he gets a little older, position your baby in front of the mirror and say, "Bye-bye" and wave. Eventually, he will imitate you. When working on names, stand in front of the mirror and say, "Who is that?" or "Kiss the baby." Finally, when he is able to walk, turn on the music and have a family dance right in front of a long mirror.

Diaper Changing Game

Game

Materials

- New diaper

Make diaper changing a game instead of a chore. Before you begin, put a clean diaper on the diapering table. Put your baby on the table. Hold your baby with your free hand while you pick up the new diaper with the other hand and use the diaper to hide your face. Move it quickly away from your face and say, "Peek-a-boo, I see you!" Repeat the activity several times, and offer a new diaper to your child. Encourage her to hold the new diaper for you. As your child gets older, she will begin imitating the peek-a-boo game.

Rolling Around

Game

Materials

- Baby's favorite toy (musical toy with lights works well)

When baby is just about to roll over, introduce her to this game. Put her on her back on a blanket on the floor. Put her favorite toy beside her, slightly out of her reach. Move behind the toy in a crouching position so that your face is close to hers. Say, "Look at me; I've got the toy. Come get me." Activate or wiggle the toy. She will naturally try to turn toward you. The first few times you play you may want to support her back and gently push to help her turn.

Middle, Middle

Materials

- None

Game

When your baby is first waking up in the morning, this is a rewarding game. You usually get to see baby's first smile. Look at him and say, "Good morning!" When you kiss him, you say, "Let me kiss your nose and kiss your toes and kiss you right in the middle!" When you say "middle," lift his nightshirt and give him a raspberry on his tummy. Soon those bright eyes will be open and the room will be filled with laughter.

Honeybee

Materials

- Food
- Spoon

Game

If you are tired of playing airplane at feeding time, try making the spoon into a honeybee. Make a buzzing noise. Fly the spoon above your baby's head, below and around the plate, right into his mouth. Tell him the honeybee is in his hive. When he takes the food off the spoon, tell him that the honeybee has got to fly! Fly into the food. Say, "Oooh! I found a flower, yum, yum, yum. Now I've got to fly back to my hive, bzzzz!"

Hollywood Stars

Materials

- Film
- Polaroid camera
- Sunglasses
- Tape player with microphone
- Cassette tape

Game

Another high-interest game to save for those grumpy days is Hollywood Stars. When you can't find anything else to interest your child, try this. Come out of your room wearing sunglasses and carrying one of the children's tape players with a microphone. Dance around the room and sing or talk into the tape player. Then rewind the tape and play it back. When your baby reaches for glasses and the microphone, snap a picture and let him see what a true Hollywood Star looks like. In all the excitement, she may forget to be grumpy.

Tears Be Gone

Materials

- Fan
- Helium balloons
- Paperweight

Game

Babies are just like we are; some days, they are just grumpy. Nothing makes them happy, and they cry for—what seems to us—no reason at all. Try this game on one of those days. Take brightly-colored helium balloons, tie them around a paperweight, and put them in front of a fan. Turn the fan on low. Position baby so he can see the balloons blowing in the breeze. Even though it is not 100% effective, usually it will fascinate even the grumpiest baby for a little while.

Note: *Popping balloons will often scare babies and undo all your hard work. Also, make sure that all deflated balloons are thrown away immediately. Babies can put deflated balloons or pieces of balloons in their mouths and choke.*

Hats

Game

Materials

- A box full of hats

Collecting the hats is half the pleasure of this game. Search through flea markets and second-hand shops to find a variety of hats. The more shapes, sizes, and colors, the better. After your shopping spree, sit with your baby in front of the mirror. Take turns trying the hats on and giggling at each other.

Jewelry Catcher

Game

Materials

- Necklace

Everyone knows that jewelry thieves have to be quiet, or they will set off the alarm. If you want to have a safeguard against your own little alarm going off in a social situation, bring or wear a strand of brightly-colored beads. When your baby starts to test the acoustics of the gathering place, move the beads within his view. Dangle them back and forth for several minutes. He will automatically reach for them and be entranced for a good five to 10 minutes, just enough time to plan your graceful exit. Try to choose a sturdy necklace—beads on the floor or in his mouth can be more hazardous than piercing cries.

Bath Time Aquarium

Game

Materials

- Plastic fish
- Sponges
- Squirting fish

Don't have time to go to the aquarium? Bring the aquarium to your baby's bath time. Before you begin his bath, you may want to change into old clothes. You could get just a little wet during this activity. Put your baby in the tub and fill it with water, fish, sponges, and squirting fish. Reach into the water and grab some of the fish. Make them look like they are swimming. Let your baby select different toys to play with and explore. When he gets to the squirting fish, duck!

Clean Nose, Clean Toes

Game

Materials

- Washcloth
- Baby doll

Play this game to encourage your baby to learn body parts and to wash herself. Let her take one of her baby dolls in the tub with her. As you wash baby, ask her to wash her baby. Name the body parts as you wash.

Where's That Sound?

Materials

- Squeaky toy

Game

Finding or localizing sound is another important milestone for your baby. Place your baby on a blanket on his back. Move behind him out of his view. Then speak sweetly to him. Watch and see if he makes some gestures, indicating he hears you. He may kick his feet, smile, move his hands, blink his eyes. Then take a squeaky toy, move it out of his sight and squeeze it. Again, notice if he seems to hear the sound. Move the toy in different areas to see how he reacts. As he develops, he should move his head in the direction of the sound.

Gym Workout

Materials

- Baby gym

Game

Do you dread a workout at the gym! Well, your baby will probably enjoy his. A baby gym is simply an activity center that encourages him to reach, grasp, and pull. You place your baby on a blanket on the floor and place the gym directly over him. Sit back and watch while he works out.

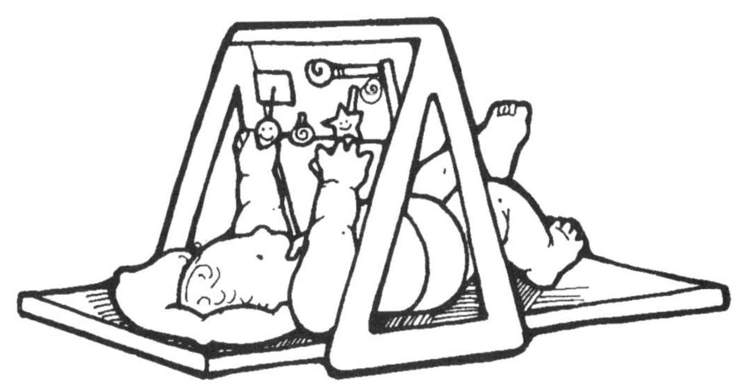

Indoor Games 6 to 11 Months

Where's the Bear?

Materials

- Stuffed animals

Game

Now that your baby is moving around, get her favorite stuffed animal. Show it to her and hide it somewhere in the room. Say, "Where's the bear?" Both of you look for the toy together.

Moving Music Box

Materials

- Music box

Game

When baby is taking a rest from all his busy activities, put her on your lap and show her a music box with moving parts. You may even rock and sing to her as she watches the parts move with each new note.

Creepy Crawly

Materials

- None

Game

Just before baby crawls, try playing this game with him. Support him under the tummy in the crawling position. Rock him back and forth, shifting his weight from his knees to his hands and back again. Say, "Creepy crawly, creepy crawly, isn't it fun how we can move! Creepy crawly!" Say "creepy" as he moves forward and "crawly" as he moves backward.

Floor Pictures

Materials

- Colored pictures
- Tape

Game

Brightly-colored pictures taped to the floor provide stimulation for babies as they crawl around the floor. Sit behind your baby supporting him. Flip through a stack of colored pictures. Pull out the ones he really seems to like. Tape them to the floor in the playroom or his bedroom. Lie on the floor as he crawls around and talk to him about the objects in the pictures. As he seems to tire of these pictures, replace them with new ones.

Elevator

Materials

- None

Game

When your baby is trying to pull up, play this game with him. Put him in a sitting position. Hold baby's hands and say, "Going up!" Gently pull him to a standing position. After he stands for a few seconds, say, "Going Down!" Gently lower him down.

Out of Reach

Materials

- Baby's favorite toys

Game

After baby starts cruising the furniture (holding onto furniture as he walks), try this game to get him to go just a little farther. Put baby at one end of the sofa and his favorite toy a few feet away. When he reaches the toy, give him a big kiss and hug and say, "You got it!" When you repeat the activity, move the toy a little farther down the sofa.

Get Me!

Materials

- None

Game

To encourage baby to go from sitting to standing, play "Get me!" Sit on the sofa with your feet up and call your baby's name. Try to get her to crawl over to the sofa. When she holds her arms out to be picked up, say "Come get me!" Coach her to pull on the sofa, helping her a little at first. When she pulls up, give her a big hug and say, "You got me!"

Find Me!

Materials

- None

Game

Another game to play when baby is pulling up and trailing furniture is Find Me! Put baby close to the end of the sofa. Hide behind that end of the sofa. Peek your head around the corner and say, "Find me!" When your baby moves close to you, hug her and say, "You found me! What a smart baby!"

Glamour Shots

Materials

- Box of dress-up clothes
- Polaroid camera

Game

On one of those rainy days, try this activity with your baby. Drag out that box of dress-up clothes you have been collecting and explore with him. Let him play with them and as he plays take Polaroid shots of him. Put up the clothes and show him the pictures of himself. Ask him to point to himself in each picture.

Hall of Fame

Materials

- Pictures of family

Game

Consider using the hallway or some part of your baby's room as a "Hall of Fame" for your family pictures. Put pictures of immediate and extended family members on the wall. As you walk down the hall with your baby or you play with him in his room, name all the people in the pictures. Ask him where Aunt Sally is or where Grandpa is and see if he will point to their pictures. If you put pictures in your baby's room, you may want to hang some at baby's eye level to encourage standing. For those pictures, you may want to use plexiglass and mount the pictures directly to the wall to avoid accidents that could occur with shattered glass or broken pieces of frame.

Decorated Plate

Materials

- Decorated plate

Game

The Decorated Plate game can be an incentive for baby to eat. Select a plate decorated with her very favorite character. Show her the plate before you fill it with food. Talk to her about the character and what it is doing. As you put food on the plate, say, "The big bear is hiding. Where is the big bear?" When you put the plate in front of baby say, "Let's find that bear. Oh look! There's an ear! Let's take another bite. Wow! There's an eye." Before long you will be able to see the entire bear or whatever character you selected.

Cereal in a Bottle

Materials

- Cereal
- Plastic bottle with wide mouth

Game

Puzzle your baby with this game. Put cereal pieces in a wide-mouthed plastic bottle with a lid. Let her figure out how to get the cereal out of the bottle. Your baby will probably work at the puzzle until she figures it out and the cereal pieces are in her mouth.

Feed the Dinosaur

Game

Materials

- Large stickers
- Objects to recycle
- Plastic containers

Get your child involved in recycling at an early age by playing this game. Place small plastic containers where he can reach them. Put stickers of his favorite characters on the front of these containers. Tell him that we have to keep the characters fed. The dinosaur likes cans, the cat likes paper, and the lion likes plastic. Whenever there is an empty can to be recycled say, "The dinosaur is hungry. Let's go feed him." Let your child place the can in the dinosaur's container. You are not only teaching your child to recycle, but you are teaching him to sort as well.

Hunting Elephants

Game

Materials

- Animal books
- Stuffed animals

When you are teaching your baby animal names, try this game. Begin by collecting stuffed animals and animal books and putting them around the two of you on the sofa or on the floor. Pick up the stuffed animal and say, "This is an elephant." Turn pages in a book and ask your child, "Is this an elephant?" "Is that an elephant?" When he points toward an elephant, say excitedly, "We've found our elephant!" Ask him if he wants to go looking for more elephants. If he says "yes," repeat the activity. If he says "no," ask him what animal he would like to hunt now. Hold up the stuffed animals and ask, "Would you like to hunt a tiger or a bear?"

Finger Shadows

Materials

- Flashlight

Game

If you want a different way to tell bedtime stories, use finger shadows. Turn out the lights in the room. Turn on the flashlight and put it behind your fingers so the shadows are cast on the wall. Tell a story using these characters. For an example of a finger shadow story, read the story below and then try to tell the story using finger shadows. You can make up hundreds of stories of your own. The sample story below will get you started.

Sample Story

Characters: *Bunny, Alligator, and Duck*

One bright day, little Bonnie Bunny went out to play with her best friend Davy Duck. The last thing Bonnie Bunny's mother told her was, "Don't go near the pond." Davy Duck loved to swim in the pond. He told Bonnie Bunny she was being silly, but she knew what her mother told her to do so she didn't go near the pond. She just watched Davy swim. All of a sudden, a big alligator came up out of the water. Davy Duck started to cry. Brandon Alligator said, "Don't be frightened. I won't hurt you, but there are other alligators who will. You need to listen to Bonnie and stay away from this pond." Davy and Bonnie left the pond. They never went back, but they played in the safe pond across the field.

Edible Clay Snakes

Materials

- Edible modeling clay

Activity

Snakes are not nearly as scary when they are made out of edible modeling clay. Since young children love to put everything in their mouths, edible modeling clay may be a little safer than store bought brands.

After you make the clay, sit down with your baby and roll a ball out of clay. Flatten the ball and lengthen it to make a fat line. Shape the line in an "S" shape and make a hissing sound. Move the line like a snake and say, "Look at the snake! It says hssssssss."

Edible Modeling Clay Recipes

Mashed Potato Dough

1 box instant mashed potatoes
very hot water (use with caution)
food coloring (optional)

Directions: Put instant mashed potatoes in a bowl. Gradually add water while stirring until the potatoes are stiff. Follow directions on the box for amounts to use. Add food coloring for color variation.

Peanut Butter Clay*

3½ cups creamy peanut butter
4 cups powdered sugar
4 cups powdered milk
3½ cups corn syrup

Directions: Blend all materials together until firm.

***Note:** If your child is allergic to peanuts, do not use this recipe. Also, be aware that children may choke on peanut butter.*

Sock People

Game

Materials

- Fabric
- Hot glue gun
- Old socks
- Permanent markers

Take those old socks and turn them into puppets. Bleach them, dry them, and decorate them with permanent markers and bits of materials. Use a glue gun to attach the pieces quickly. These socks make great storytellers, especially at bedtime. Put her in her crib and let the puppets perform for her over the railing. Be careful not to let her play with these because the glue and chemicals may be harmful to her.

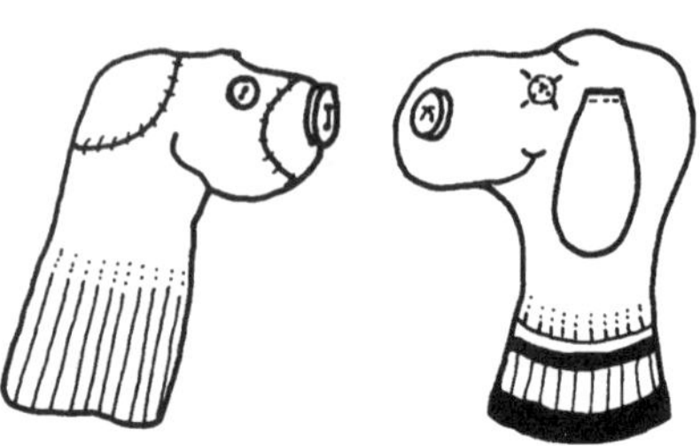

Balloon Village

Game

Materials

- Clear helium balloons
- Felt pens

If baby is sick, this may be an activity to make her feel better. Create a balloon village so that she will have something to look at while you rock her or she lies in her crib. Use several different kinds of brightly-colored balloons. Draw faces on them with permanent felt pens and tie them to paperweights. Put them within her view, but not her touch, around the room. The colorful funny faces may make her feel a little better.

Indoor Games 12 to 18 Months

Mimic Me!

Materials

- None

Game

At this age, babies naturally mimic adults. Sit down on the floor with your baby. Act silly: stick out your tongue, clap your hands, stomp your feet, and make silly faces. When she tires of this game, turn the tables on her and mimic her.

Missing Word

Materials

- Book

Game

When sitting down to read baby's favorite book, try leaving out a word or putting the wrong word in its place. See if baby notices and corrects you.

Mine/Yours

Materials

- A toy of his
- Something of yours

Game

Your baby is beginning to learn the differences between mine and yours. Take his favorite object and say, "Your ball." Hand it to him. Get something of yours and say, "My scarf." Repeat this activity several times. When he becomes more comfortable with this game, turn the tables on him and say "My ball, your scarf." Expect him to correct you quickly.

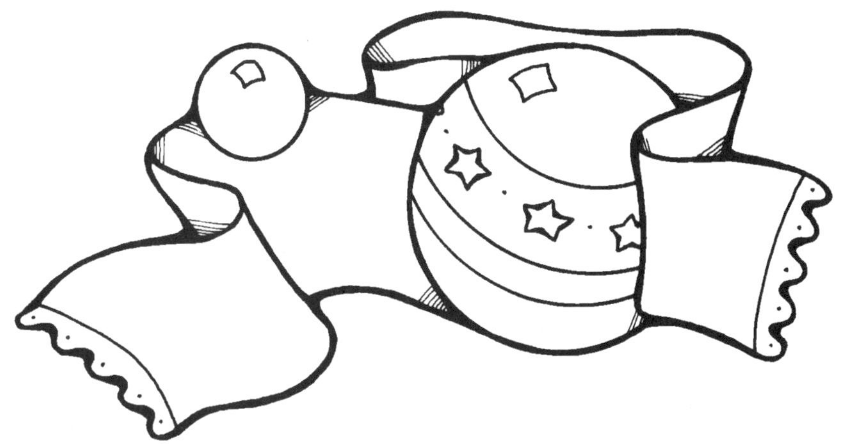

Flying Saucer

Materials

- Glow-in-the-dark Frisbee

Game

When you want to have a little fun, grab a glow-in-the-dark Frisbee, put your baby in the crib, and turn off all the lights. Hold the Frisbee in your hand and move it around the room like a flying saucer. If you're careful, you can even toss it gently across the room. Baby will have fun watching this glowing saucer.

Animal Crackers

Materials

- Animal crackers
- Tape with animal songs

Game

Make snack time a game. Line up some of the animal crackers and name them. Put on a musical tape or CD that names animals. Let your baby find and eat the animals that are named in the songs.

Finger Puppets

Materials

- Old gloves
- Markers
- Pieces of material

Game

Make a pair of old gloves into imaginary friends for your baby. Decorate the fingers so that they look like animals or people by using markers to make their faces and adding pieces of materials to make their outfits. Then at mealtime, slip the glove on one hand and keep the rest of your arm hidden. Surprise your baby by having the fingers start talking to him about all the foods on his plate. Let them name the foods and talk about how yummy they are. Have the puppets ask him to name the foods and to take a big bite just for them. When he takes a bite, let the fingers scream with delight.

Another wonderful time to use finger puppets is at bedtime. Let the bedtime story come to life with this little troupe of finger actors.

Dressing Your Parts

Game

Materials

- Clothes

As you dress your baby, play the Dressing Your Parts game. As you put the shirt over her head, say, "Here comes your shirt, over your eyes, your nose, your mouth, and your chin. Wow! I can see your face. Where are your arms?" Reach in the sleeves and pull them out. "Here they are! Here come your pants over your toes, your legs, and zip, they're on!"

Refrigerator Face

Game

Materials

- Magnets
- Felt pens
- Paper

When your child is learning his body parts, get out a large sheet of white paper. With a non-toxic marker, draw the outline of a face. Stick the picture on the refrigerator with four magnets. Make sure the picture is at eye level for your child. Draw and cut out hair, ears, mouth, eyebrows, and nose or cut them out of various magazines. Attach one body part to each magnet, using rolled tape. (By using rolled tape, you frequently can change the pictures on the magnets.) Put the pictures on the face. Ask baby to get the nose and hand it to you. Then ask him to remove the eyes, etc., until he has handed you all the body parts. When he can do that with no difficulty, reverse the game. Have him place the parts on the face. Change the eyes, noses, and eyebrows to make the pictures look funny. **Note:** Be careful to watch baby closely while he is holding each body piece. Also, remove the game when you aren't directly supervising baby so he will not be tempted to remove pieces and put them in his mouth.

Rice Play

Game

Materials

- Cups
- Plastic tub with lid
- Rice
- Scoops

Fill a plastic tub halfway full with rice. Throw in some plastic cups and scoops. Put a towel down on the kitchen floor and put the plastic container on the towel. Get down on the floor next to your baby. You can have hours of fun pouring rice into containers, hiding toys in the rice then watching your baby find them, and naming the objects she finds. Rice provides much of the fun and texture experience of sand without all the mess. Of course, as with any object, be careful that baby does not put the rice in her mouth. When you're finished, simply sweep up the fallen pieces, snap the plastic lid back on, and save the rice for another day. Make sure to bundle up the towel with any stray rice that might be slippery under foot.

Scribbling to Music

Game

Materials

- Music
- CD player/stereo
- Paper
- Big crayons

In the mood to be creative? Try this game. Select your favorite music. You may want to get a variety of music: fast, slow, mellow. Get out big sheets of paper and big crayons. Put your child in a seat that makes it easy for her to reach the paper. Flip on the music. Take turns scribbling on the same sheet of paper. Try to color to the beat of the music. Draw lots of lines and circles and see if she will imitate you. At the end of the game, you will have some great refrigerator displays.

Laser Show

Materials

- Christmas tree lights
- Music

Game

When you have some time and want to do something especially fun, pull out the colored Christmas tree lights and put on some of your or your baby's favorite music. Put baby in his crib, turn on the music, and plug in the lights. Move the lights to the music and create a laser show just for baby.

Hidey-Hole Games

Materials

- Chairs
- Sheets
- Boxes

Game

Young children love to find hiding places. A great rainy day game is to play in hidey-holes. Pull a few chairs together and drape a sheet over them to make a tent. If you have boxes, you may want to cut doors in them and connect them to the tent. Let your baby explore the tunnels. Then you may want to crawl in with him. Play a game of Hide and Seek or Chase through the maze, or just have a rainy day tea party in a box.

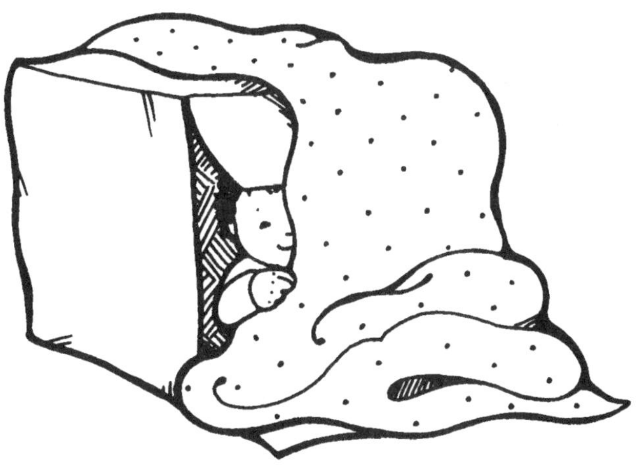

Kitchen Cabinet Games

Materials

- Pots and pans
- Cans

Game

Kitchen cabinets provide some of the best no-cost entertainment! Before you allow your baby to play in the cabinets, make sure that you have safety-proofed even the cabinets you don't want him to explore. After playing these games, if he didn't want to get into the cabinets before, he will now. Sit down beside him on the kitchen floor. Help him pull out pots and pans and plastic containers. Fit smaller containers into large ones. Then give him a turn. Take cans and make a fence around both of you. Look at the labels on the cans and ask him to name the items for you. When he gets a little older, take turns sorting colors or counting cans. Kitchen cabinets provide an entertaining and educational playground.

Train Time

Materials

- Electric or battery-operated trains
- Engineer caps

Game

Who can resist a little red caboose flying around the track? Few adults and even fewer children. Lay the tracks down. Put on your engineer caps, get in the middle of the tracks with your baby in your lap, and flip the switch! You and your child will have hours of fun playing co-engineers.

Action Words and Animal Shows

Materials

- TV animal show

Game

Turn high-interest TV shows into interactive games. While watching a high-action animal show, ask your baby what the animal is doing. Answer the question for her. Ask her the question again later. Eventually, she will be able to say some of her verbs.

TV Characters

Materials

- TV

Game

Besides their parents, TV characters are often very special to children. Some of their first words might be references to their favorite characters. Take advantage of their natural love for these characters. When your baby's favorite show comes on, take off one morning. Don't go wash the dishes; watch his show with her. When the music comes on, sing and dance around the room together. Both of you will get to enjoy the morning even more.

Please Bring Me

Game

Materials

- Basket of toys

A game to play with your child to work on following directions and identifying objects is Please Bring Me. Put a basket of toys a few feet away from where you are sitting. Look at your baby and say, "Please bring me the doggie." If he brings you the doggie, give him a big hug and say, "Thank you." If he doesn't bring you the right toy, tell him "Thank you, that is a bunny. Let me help you find the doggie." When he finds the doggie, give him a big hug.

Picking Up Toys

Game

Materials

- Toys

Teach baby that taking care of the house can be fun by playing this game. Put on some peppy music and take turns picking up toys. Dance around the room and drop them in the toy box. Soon the room will be clean, and both you and baby will be in a good mood.

Building Dreams

Materials

- Stacking blocks

Game

Another classic toy is the stacking block. Stacking blocks are real winners. They help your baby use the small muscles in her fingers, and they also help her develop creativity. Put the container of stacking blocks on the floor. Your child will enjoy dumping them out and putting them back in the container. You can play, too. Just take turns! Also, you may want to show her how she can bang the blocks together to make noises. Bang the blocks to the rhythm of some favorite music. Finally, show her how one block can be stacked on top of another. As she develops, you and she can work on building your dreams.

Block Stacking

Materials

- Stacking Blocks

Game

Use the handmade stacking blocks (page 19) or use sponge or wooden stacking blocks. On a rainy afternoon, spread them out all over the floor. Show your baby how to stack one block on top of another. When your baby first begins stacking blocks, she will probably just stack one block on top of another. Make a really tall stack for baby and then let her knock them over. She will love this game and will want you to restack the blocks time and again. An extension to this game is to place a noisy object like a bell at the top of the stack so that when she knocks the stack over, the bell will make a noise.

Family Album

Game

Materials

- Family album

Now that you've made your album (page 20), you can use it a variety of ways. Bedtime and rainy days are always good. Sit down with your baby and put him on your lap. Let him turn the pages to work on those little muscle skills. Name all the people in the album. Go back through, name members of your family, and ask him to point to the pictures. When he gets really good at this, hold the closed book on your lap and ask him to find Uncle Ted or Aunt Louise. You may be amazed at how quickly he can find their pages.

Reading the Family Story

Game

Materials

- Family story album

Make reading the family story a pleasant time. On a calm night when you don't feel rushed, sit down with your baby. Let him look at the book, picture by picture. Ask him to name all the family members. Tell him what they are doing. Don't be surprised if the memories associated with this book become so special that it becomes one of your favorite keepsakes.

Family Reading Night

Materials

- Big blanket
- Variety of books

Game

Gather the whole family together. Turn off the TV and the computer, and turn on the answering machine. Drag out the beanbag chair, put a blanket on the floor, and have fun reading as a family. Even though your baby can't read, he is never too young for books! There are a wide variety of books that squeak, feel funny, and even talk. Have several on his blanket and explore with him. Older kids may want to help baby read his books.

Bowling

Materials

- Child's bowling set

Game

Children's bowling sets have been around for years. They transform an empty hallway into an activity center. Set up the plastic pins at the end of your hall. Take turns rolling the plastic ball toward the pins. When you first begin, let baby stand very close, so he can hit at least one pin. As he grows, he can move further back. If you don't want to buy a bowling set, fill 20-ounce drink bottles half full of water. Screw the caps on tight and set up your pins. To make the bottles look more interesting, use clear soda bottles. Color the water with different colors of food coloring. When your baby gets tired of bowling, make a game out of having baby find different-colored bottles and bring them to you or knocking different-colored bottles down.

Baby Air Hockey

Materials

- Plastic coaster or big plastic truck or car
- Smooth surface table

Game

Need an indoor activity that everyone in the family will enjoy? Play a modified version of air hockey. Place baby at one end of the table. To begin with, someone in the family may need to stand on baby's end of the table to help her. Put the plastic coaster on the table in front of you. Push it toward baby. You should try to push it off baby's edge of the table. Let baby have a turn. She should try to push it off your edge of the table. With older children, you can keep score. Everytime the coaster goes off the table edge on the opponent's side, the one pushing the coaster gets a point. With baby, just enjoy pushing the coaster back and forth and watching her laugh. Later, try the game with a toy car or truck.

Cereal Box Games

Materials

- Different types of cereal boxes

Game

You may never have thought of cereal boxes as terrific toys, but they really are! They are light so your baby can carry them around with no danger of hurting herself. Just shake out the last remaining crumbs, tape the tops of the boxes, and you have a set of blocks. You can help baby turn the boxes on their sides and stack them.

Also, cereal boxes usually have bright and colorful pictures on them. While eating breakfast, you can play a game of "name that picture" with your baby.

Finally, you can use cereal boxes for matching and sorting activities. Help your baby sort them by type or size. Or cut out the pictures on the front and make these pictures into big matching cards.

Toilet Paper Tube Zoo

Materials

- Toilet paper tubes
- Markers
- Construction paper

Game

Toilet paper tubes are other items that you may not want to throw in the trash. Spend an afternoon with your baby making animals out of toilet paper tubes. Decorate them with paper and markers. When you have a collection of animals, put them in a big box and call it a zoo. Then you have animals to use in naming games or in telling stories to your child.

Keep Away

Game

Materials

- Soft indoor ball

If you have a playroom or a large space without a lot of collectibles, indoor ball can be fun—especially on those rainy days. Keep Away may be played with two people (or more with minor rule changes).

If just you and your baby play, sit down on the floor in front of your baby. Gently toss the ball from one hand to the other, giving your baby a chance to grab the ball.

If more than the two of you want to play, have everyone sit on the floor with your baby in the middle. Toss the ball from person to person, just over your baby's head. When he catches it, cheer and start the game again.

Indoor Basketball

Game

Materials

- Baby basketball
- Small plastic hoop

Several toy companies have created indoor basketball hoops, just the right size for your baby. They also manufacture miniature basketballs, just right for little hands. Set up one of these in your playroom or child's bedroom. Take turns throwing the ball through the hoop. You may be surprised; she may be better at this game than you are!

Sticky Words

Materials

- Album
- Variety of stickers

Game

Want those new words to stick with your baby? Start a sticker album. Collect a variety of stickers that are common animals and objects. Everytime your child learns a new word, try to find a sticker that represents that word and stick it in your child's album. When you get a page full of stickers, review the words by pointing to the stickers and getting your child to name them.

Scavenger Hunt

Materials

- Five items your baby can name

Game

Think of five items that your baby can name. They should be easy for him to pick up and move. Make sure they are in their usual places. Ask your baby to find each item and bring it to you. You may be surprised at how observant he has been. He may be able to find some items before other members in your family can.

Rubby, Dub, Dub, Books in the Tub

Materials

- Plastic tub books

Game

Books are not only fun on dry land, but they are fun in the tub, too. Get a couple of plastic books and put them in the tub with your baby. Let her explore the way the books bend and move in the water. If you're lucky enough to find a plastic book with sea animals, match floating tub animals with pictures in the book.

Floating Letters and Numbers

Materials

- Tub letters and numbers

Game

Floating letters and numbers stick to the sides of the tub and then pull right off. Even though your baby doesn't recognize her letters and numbers yet, she will still have a great time with the variety of shapes and colors these provide. Help her sort the numbers and letters into colors or just help her make designs on the tub!

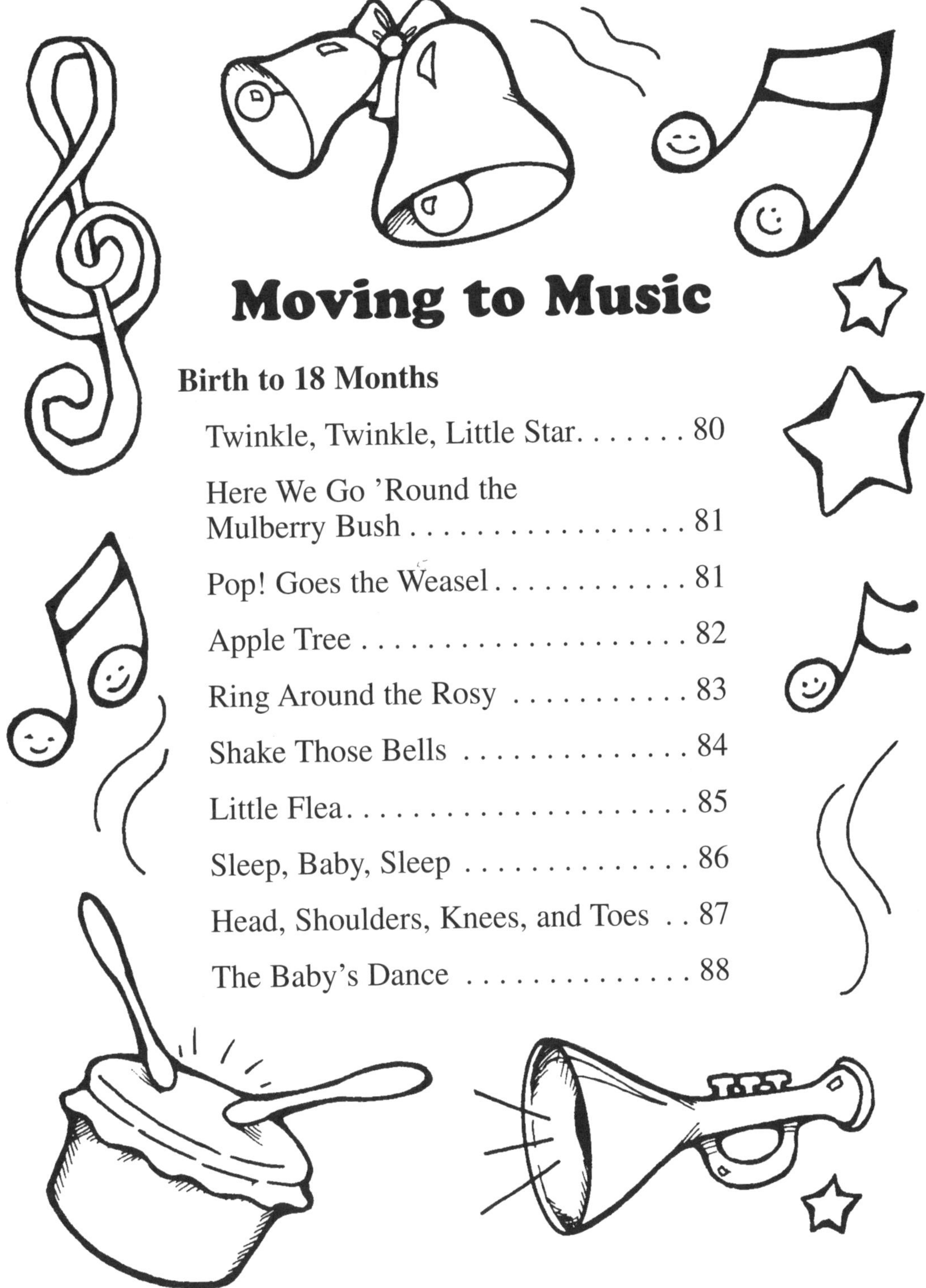

Moving to Music

Birth to 18 Months

Twinkle, Twinkle, Little Star

Materials

- Cake sprinkles
- Star cookie cutter
- Sugar cookie dough

Twinkle, twinkle, little star,
How I wonder what you are,
Up above the world so high,
Like a diamond in the sky.
Twinkle, twinkle, little star,
How I wonder what you are.

Make an evening special by sprinkling it with stars. Take your baby outside on a clear night and show him the stars in the sky. Tell him that you are going inside to make stars that the two of you can actually eat. Place baby in a seat so that he can see you make the star cookies. Pop open a can of cookie dough and roll it out. Cut out stars with a cookie cutter and decorate them with sprinkles. Talk to him about the shape of the cookies and shiny stars as you cook. Pop the cookies in the oven and in about 10 minutes, you will have a basket full of warm, tasty stars. Take your baby outside and eat cookies and milk underneath the stars. When you're finished, sing *Twinkle, Twinkle Little Star* to end your special evening.

Here We Go 'Round the Mulberry Bush

Materials

- Basket
- Berry bush

Here we go round the ________ bush,

the ______________ bush, the _________ bush,

Here we go round the ________ bush,

so early in the morning.

While you are picking berries with your baby, sing *Here We Go 'Round the Mulberry Bush*, but substitute the name of your bush for "mulberry" (blueberry, raspberry, etc.)

Pop! Goes the Weasel

Materials

- none

All around the cobbler's bench,

The monkey chased the weasel.

The monkey thought 'twas all in fun.

Pop! goes the weasel.

Feel like dancing? Add a little additional movement to this old classic. Grab your baby's hands and sing the first three lines as the two of you go around in a circle. When you sing *Pop! Goes the Weasel*, gently grab your baby by the waist and raise her above your head.

Apple Tree

Materials

- Fruit tree

Another song to sing while you are picking fruit is *Apple Tree*. Again, substitute the fruit you are actually picking for "apple."

Way up high in the apple tree,

Two little apples smiled at me.

I shook that tree as hard as I could,

Down came the apples,

Mmmmm, they were good!

Ring Around the Rosy

Materials

- Tambourine
- Rattle
- Drum

Ring around the rosy,

Pocket full of posies,

Ashes, ashes,

We all fall down!

On a day you don't mind a noisy game, try this one. Take your baby outside with a box of musical toys: a tambourine, a rattle, and a drum. Sing *Ring Around the Rosy* as you march in a circle and beat, ring, or rattle. When you get to the last line, fall down, and shake, rattle, or sing as hard as you can.

Shake Those Bells

Materials

- Rattles with bells
- Bells on a band

Shake those bells and shake them high,
Shake those bells and shake them low,
Shake those bells and shake them high,
Shake those bells, around you go!

At this age babies love to make noise, and they like to see their effect on their world. Shake Those Bells is a game that will allow them to do both. Round up a variety of bells. You may have some rattles with bells on them. You may even have some bells left from the winter holidays. Put them in a pile in front of baby and you and sing *Shake Those Bells*. As you sing, follow the directions in the song.

Little Flea

Materials

- Washcloth

Creeping, creeping, little flea,

Up my leg and past my knee.

To my tummy, on he goes

Past my chin and to my nose,

Now he's creeping down my chin,

To my tummy once again,

Down my leg and past my knee,

To my toe, that little flea. Gotcha!

If you enjoy singing in the shower, see if you don't enjoy singing in the tub with your baby even more. Put water in the tub and put your baby in.

Take the washcloth and drape it over your index finger and your thumb. Make a gentle biting motion with your fingers over the toes, up the legs, past the knee, and to the tummy of your baby. Take a big breath and then continue singing and moving the cloth past his chin up to his nose, and then start down again. When you say "Gotcha," grab his big toe and shake.

Sleep, Baby, Sleep

Materials

- Rocker

Sleep, baby, sleep,

Your father tends the sheep,

Your mother shakes the dreamland tree,

Down falls a little dream for thee

Sleep, baby, sleep.

Sometimes nothing is sweeter than rocking your baby and singing to her. Take your baby in your arms, rock gently back and forth, and sing quietly to her. If she is fussy when you hold her lengthwise, try holding her head on your shoulder and feet in your lap so that she can see as you rock.

Head, Shoulders, Knees, and Toes

Materials

- Diaper

Heads, shoulders, knees, and toes,

Knees and toes,

Heads, shoulders, knees, and toes,

Knees and toes,

And eyes and ears and mouth and nose.

Heads, shoulders, knees, and toes,

Knees and toes.

This little ditty is a great one to sing during diaper changing. First, sing the song while placing your hands on your head and wiggling your fingers. Put one finger on your nose and wiggle your nose. If you are changing her on the sofa or bed, place your foot beside her and wiggle your toes. Sing the song again, but touch her head and wiggle her nose and toes. Playing this game will not only keep her entertained but will also help her learn her body parts.

The Baby's Dance

Materials

- None

Dance, little baby, dance up high,

Dance, little baby, I'm nearby,

Crow and caper, caper and crow,

There, little baby, there you go.

Up to the ceiling, down to the ground,

Backward and forward, round and round.

Dance little baby, and we shall sing

With a merry song of ring a-ding ding.

Lie on your back. Put your baby in a sitting position on your stomach. When you sing, "dance up high," gently raise your baby above your head. When you say, "up to the ceiling," lift him a little higher, and then gently lower him down when you say "down to the ground." He should now be sitting on your stomach again. Move him a little way backwards and a little way forwards. Then take his arms and have them go around each other. Don't be surprised if he wants the song repeated.

Outdoor Games Birth to 11 Months

Birth to 5 Months

6 to 11 Months

Stroller Talking

Game

Materials

- Stroller

This is a pleasant game for both you and your baby. Put your baby in the stroller and take her outside to experience a variety of sights and sounds. Stroll her around the yard or down the street, but don't stop there. You'll miss out on all the fun! Talk to her as you stroll. Name objects that you pass, and when you see something really exciting, like a dog, squirrel, or a patch of brightly-colored flowers, pick her up and show her. What a wonderful way to bond, help her build her language skills, and get your daily exercise.

Blanket Play

Game

Materials

- Blanket
- Cap
- Sunscreen

Another game to play outside is Blanket Play. Find a shady spot, spread a blanket on the ground and sit beside your baby. Just putting the sunscreen on him can be fun. He will enjoy the attention and your touch. After he has his sunscreen on, put him on his back and talk to him about the sky, the birds, and the tree tops. In a few minutes, let him see the world from a different view. You may even want to position him close to the blanket's edge so he can reach for and feel the grass. Just remember that babies have delicate skin that burns easily, so don't forget the sunscreen and the cap!

Bubble Game

Game

Materials:

- Bubbles

One inexpensive and high-interest outdoor game is the Bubble Game. Take a big bottle of bubbles outside with your baby. Blow bubbles slightly above your baby's head and let him chase them and try to pop them. When he tires of this game, let him practice blowing bubbles.

Flying Kites

Game

Materials

- Kites

It doesn't have to be March to have fun with kites! This is another great activity that you can do just with baby or with the whole family. Get kites of different shapes and sizes. Go to any open area, get baby's kite flying, and then tie the string to the stroller. Move the stroller to keep the kite flying. It may not stay up for long, but baby will enjoy it. Of course, just watching everyone else fly their kites is an activity that both you and baby can enjoy.

Finding Treasure

Game

Materials

- Spray paint
- Pine cones

When your baby is somewhere between six and eleven months, she will probably begin to search for hidden objects. Easter egg hunts are great in the spring, but what do you do the rest of the year? Start by taking your baby outside to collect pine cones. Just collecting them can be entertaining when you have company. Then while baby naps, spray-paint five or six of them bright colors. Let them dry. Hide them behind bushes, around trees, in the grass. Take your baby outside and help her find them. Soon she will be hiding them for you!

Collecting Memories

Game

Materials

- Basket

For another treasure hunt, try taking a basket with you on your morning or evening walk. As you meander down your usual path, look for new or unusual items. Find different-shaped rocks, pretty colored leaves, delicate wildflowers, and put them in your basket. You will notice that your baby will begin picking up treasures, too. When you get home, take everything out of your basket and arrange it on a table. Talk to your baby about each item. Select one object that you especially like and put it in a display case. When your baby grows older, each piece will be a memory of time shared together.

Wagon Train

Game

Materials

- Wagon

This game is fun to play all year long, but the cool weather may make it more fun for you—since you have to pull the wagon! Get a little wagon and throw a couple of pillows and a blanket in it, just to make it extra comfy. Pull the wagon up to the door and say, "All aboard!" Help your baby get in the wagon and say, "Train is pulling out." Take her for a spin around the yard, making "choo-choo" sounds. When you get back to the door, say "Home station!" Help her get out. Next time, you may ask her if she wants a traveling partner. A doll or stuffed animal is always good company.

Making a Zoo

Game

Materials

- Stuffed animals

Think the toy animals need an outing? Take a few outside and try to create a habitat for them. Put the monkeys in the tree, the lion in the grass, the plastic fish in the kiddy pool. Pretend to take your little one to the zoo. Talk to him about the animals and where they live. In this zoo, you don't have to worry about the animals being cranky or biting. Just enjoy a carefree afternoon. You may even pretend to feed peanuts to the elephant.

Touch the Sky

Materials

- Baby swing

Game

The most popular piece of equipment in the park is often the swing. Take your baby to the park and pick out a baby-sized swing just for him. Push him, and as he goes up, say, "Up, up, up to the sky!" As he goes down, say, "Down, down, down to the ground." Remember, before you push him, make sure he is secured in the swing.

Foot Catcher

Materials

- Baby swing

Game

When baby gets used to swinging, stand in front of him for a few minutes instead of behind. Or, if another family member is with you, have one of you stand behind and the other in front. When baby's feet swing up toward you, briefly grab them and say in a gruff voice, "I'm the foot catcher, and I'll get your toes." After a quick tickle, let go and wait for the giggle.

Outdoor Games 12 to 18 Months

Drawing Sticks

Materials

- Dirt
- Water

Game

Find an area where there isn't much grass. Get two sticks and give one to your baby. Show him how you can draw pictures in the dirt. Let him draw. Then try to get him to name objects you draw. This no-cost game will be a favorite for years.

Mud Pies

Materials

- Dirt
- Stick

Game

All it takes is a little water and dirt to make a fun game of mud pies. You have to be willing to get a little dirty, though! Put on your oldest clothes and go out with baby right after a spring rain. If it's not raining, create your own mudhole with a water hose. Sit down next to the puddle, put your hands in the mud, and "squish" it between your fingers. Take a handful of mud and pat it into a cake shape. Make several cakes. Put the cakes in a line, and both of you can admire your work.

Sidewalk Scribble

Materials

- Colorful sidewalk chalk
- Sidewalk

Game

Sidewalk chalk comes in big, colorful pieces. Take your favorite color and scribble on a block of sidewalk. Let your baby have a turn, but be careful he doesn't try to eat the chalk. If you don't think he is old enough to handle the chalk, put him in a stroller. Pull him up beside you. Draw simple pictures and encourage him to name them.

Outdoor Paintings

Materials

- Paper
- Finger paint

Game

Painting with little ones is not a neat activity so you may have more fun if you take it outside. Put down large pieces of paper on picnic tables or on the sidewalk. Make sure both you and your baby are in your play clothes. Squirt one color of finger paint onto the paper and show your baby how to smear the paint. Squirt a different color onto the paper and continue to paint with her. You may want to turn on the music for a little additional fun while you paint. When you're finished, just hose off before you go inside.

Streamers in the Breeze

Materials

- Streamers
- Stick or plastic bracelet

Game

Want an excuse to play outside on a spring day? Play Streamers in the Breeze. Tie brightly-colored cloth streamers to the end of a stick or a bracelet. Go outside with baby and run, letting the brightly-colored streamers trail behind you.

Pinwheel Delight

Materials

- Pinwheels

Game

Buy or make a variety of pinwheels. Mount them on top of your fence. Watch them turn as the wind moves them. They are even more fun if you get them in different colors. Save one pinwheel for baby to hold. She will enjoy blowing it and watching the pinwheel turn.

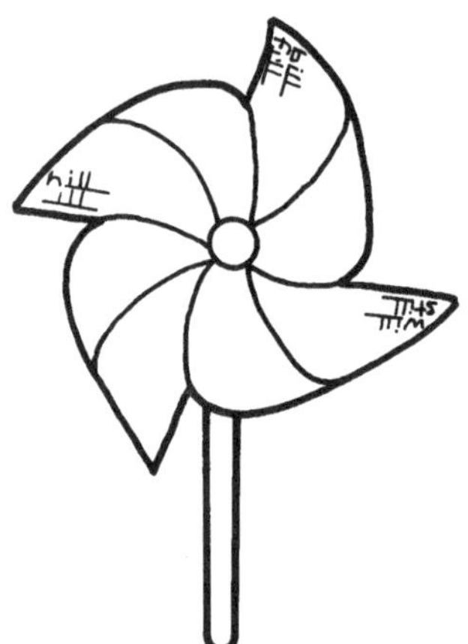

Keep on Trucking

Game

Materials

- 2 battery-operated trucks

Everyone in the family will enjoy this game. On a pretty Saturday afternoon, take two battery-operated trucks and your family outside. Let everyone, including grandma, have a turn at playing with the switches. Even very young children easily operate switches, and it is a great activity for working on those fine motor skills. After everyone has had a turn learning how to operate the trucks, line up the trucks. Mark a starting and finishing line in the dirt, and let family members race against each other. The only down side to this game is everyone will want his or her own truck by the end of the day! (Don't worry if there are only two of you. You won't have to share your truck.)

Airplanes

Game

Materials

- Different paper

Slightly breezy days are the best days for paper airplanes. Lure everyone away from their chores and the TV and take them outside. Give them sheets of brightly-colored paper and let them make their own airplanes. Little ones will need help, but they still can participate. Then let the airplanes go. The different-colored airplanes will add to the excitement and keep family members from fighting over planes. If you and your baby are the only two playing, you may want to make several planes out of different colors and alternate throwing them.

Scarves

Game

Materials

- Brightly-colored scarves
- Battery-operated radio or tape player and cassettes

As you shop, look for long, brightly-colored scarves on sale. When you have several, line up everyone and give each person a different-colored scarf. Turn on the music and dance around the yard, letting the scarves trail behind you. Throw them up and catch them. Throw them up and let them float to the ground. Bend over and wave them between your legs. Let the music lead you and have fun!

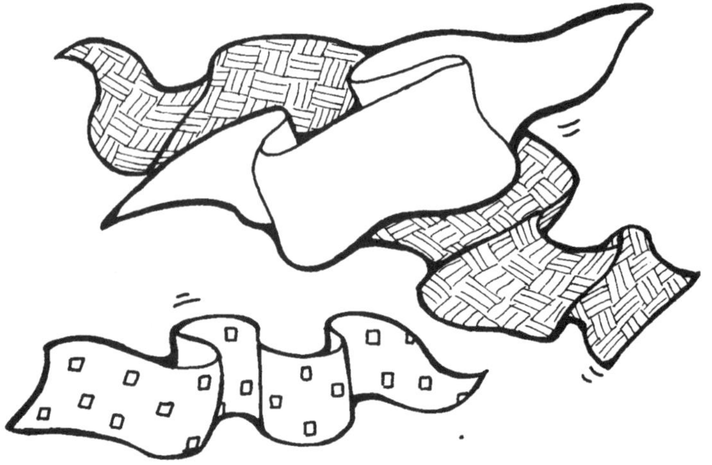

Marching Band

Game

Materials

- Band instruments
- Battery-operated radio

Put a little sand in a plastic milk jug, sew bells to the end of old gloves, make a drum out of a round oatmeal box. Take the radio outside and you and your baby can take turns playing all the instruments to any music you choose.

Obstacle Course

Game

Materials

- Boxes
- Old tires
- Plastic barrels
- Plastic slide

Feeling athletic? This is a good game for you. Find a spot in the yard and make an obstacle course. Use boxes and tires to step over, a plastic slide to climb up and slide down, and if you are really adventurous, a mud puddle to hop over. Go through the course with your baby. Be careful to hold her hand when necessary. You may even want to start with one "obstacle." When she masters that skill, add a more challenging piece. How about laying down a towel to roll on?

Step Way Up

Game

Materials

- Steps

An important skill for your child to master is going up and down steps, so make a game out of it! Usually, the most important outdoor steps for your child to learn to maneuver are those going to your front door. If your home doesn't have outdoor steps, you may want to help your child climb steps leading to play areas or to play equipment. Just make sure the first steps he tries are not too narrow, deep, or many. Three or four steps are really enough for the first few attempts. Take your baby's favorite toy and put it on the top step. Hold your child's hand as he starts to climb. You will be surprised at how quickly he masters this skill when there is something he wants at the other end!

Milk Carton Kick

Materials

- Empty milk carton
- Sand

Game

Instead of throwing that empty milk carton in the trash, make it into a game piece. Fill it about one quarter full with sand. Close and tape the top. Now, take a stick and draw one line in the dirt, walk 10 paces, and draw another line in the dirt. Start behind one line and count the number of kicks it takes to get the milk carton over the second line. The more times you and your baby play the game, the fewer kicks it should take. Just remember to give your baby her turns!

Stars in a Jar

Materials

- Jar with holes in lid
- Lightning bugs (fireflies)

Game

Stars in a Jar is an old fashioned game but one that children always enjoy. Take your baby outside on an early summer evening and let him watch the lightning bugs. Help him catch a few and put them in a glass jar with holes in the lid. When you put him to bed, put the jar out of his reach, but where he can still see it. He will fall asleep watching tiny stars twinkling in the dark.

After he is fast asleep, you may want to give the lightning bugs their freedom, so they can continue to work their magic for children and adults.

Mailbox Chatter

Materials

- Mailbox

Game

If you have never thought of a mailbox as a toy, try this game. Take your baby on a walk. Stop by the mailbox. Open the door and talk into it. Let your baby hear the echoes. He will immediately begin chattering in the mailbox to hear the echoes. This game is especially good for words you are having trouble getting him to pronounce.

Bean Bag Toss

Materials

- Bean bags
- Cardboard backboard

Game

This is an old game with a new twist. Transform beans and squares of materials into beanbags by sewing three sides of the materials together to make a pouch. Pour beans in the pouch so that it is half full. Then sew the top closed. You have your beanbags; now, all you need is a backboard.

You can buy backboards, or you can make your own. All you need is a large piece of cardboard. If you are artistic, draw the face of your child's favorite cartoon character on the cardboard. Paint it with bright colors. After it dries, cut out the mouth of the character.

Make supports that allow the cardboard figure to stand independently. Let your baby stand up close to the figure and drop in the beanbag. As he develops, encourage him to step back farther and try tossing the bean bag into the mouth. It is a fun game that will last for years.

Jump the Cracks

Materials

- None

Game

To add a little more excitement to walking down the sidewalk, play Jump the Cracks. When you get to a crack, grab your baby under her arms and help her jump over the crack. If she lands on the crack, go back and try it again. Warning: She will probably want to play this game as long as your back can stand it.

Catch Me!

Materials

- None

Game

With all these new games, don't forget the old standby: chase. You yell, "Catch me if you can" and run a little bit. When baby catches you, turn around and chase her. This game works really well outside because you can hide around the corners of the house. She will love it when you step out and say, "Gotcha!" You may even want to grab her and swing her around before you begin again. If you live near the street, stay close to her so that she doesn't run out into the road.

Spoon Tunnel

Materials

- Sand
- Spoons

Game

Play in the sandbox and teach your baby how to handle a spoon all at the same time. Get two spoons and take your baby outside to the sandbox. If you don't have a sandbox, try keeping damp sand in a large plastic container with a lid. Store it on your porch or garage for easy access. Give your baby a spoon, and you take a spoon. Then dig tunnels until your spoons touch. Drop your spoon, grab his fingers and say, "Gotcha!" He will squeal and squirm to get away but will be eager to begin the game again.

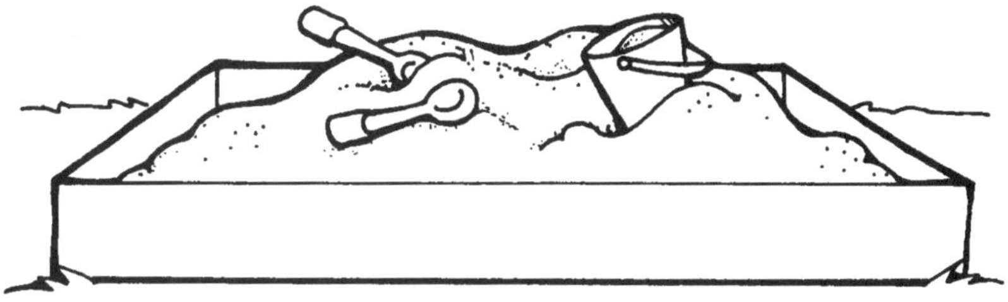

Cowbell Ring

Materials

- Cowbell or any large bell

Game

On one of those days when nothing bothers you, play Cowbell Ring. Put the bell on a stump, table, or anything low enough for your baby to reach. Pretend to race for the bell. Let him get it and spend a few minutes ringing it. Then begin the game again.

Glowing Ball

Materials

- Fluorescent ball

Game

Take advantage of the cooler summer evenings by playing Glowing Ball. Several types of fluorescent balls are on the market. Some are bright orange, and some even have big, bright yellow stars. Go out after dark. Let your baby stand directly in front of you and roll the ball to her. Encourage her to roll it back. She will love to watch the glowing ball roll!

Follow the Leader

Materials

- None

Game

Babies love to mimic! Play a game of follow the leader with your baby. Walk around the yard with your baby following you. Touch your nose, sit down, and watch your baby follow your lead.

Blowing Dandelions

Materials

- Dandelions

Game

Dandelions are nature's bubbles. Pick one and blow. Your baby will be delighted as the white fluff goes floating through the air. Go on a hunt for more dandelions. Pretend to race him for them. If you look disappointed when he wins, he may even share one of his dandelions with you.

Daisy Petals

Materials

- A daisy patch

Game

Go back to your childhood by playing this game. Pick a daisy and sit down in the grass by your baby. Pluck off a petal and say, "He loves me." Pluck off another petal and say, "He loves me not." Of course, you may have to fudge a little, but you always want your game to end with "He loves me." When you pluck your last petal, give your baby a big hug. Of course, your baby knows everyone loves him, so the game may have no meaning for him, but he will enjoy plucking the petals anyway.

Pine Cone Toss

Materials

- Pine cones
- Target

Game

Make a simple game out of pine cones and a big target. You can either buy the target or make one out of a white poster board and black and red markers. If you have access to a laminating machine, you may want to laminate the poster after you are finished so it will last longer. Some teacher supply stores have laminating machines for use, or you can also use laminating paper if your target is not too large. After the target is completed and attached to a tree (at an 18-month-old's height), take a few minutes to run around and collect pine cones. Throw the pine cones at the target and see how many times you can hit the big red center. Let baby stand up close.

Flower, Shrub, and Tree

Materials

- None

Game

To help teach your child sizes and categories, play this game. As you walk around the park, name flowers, shrubs, and trees. Walk back around the same area and see if your child can name the same flowers, shrubs, and trees. Play the game in your own backyard for practice. Pose these questions, "Which is bigger, the apple tree or the daisy bush?" or "What color are the flowers by the big rock?"

Balls, Balls, and More Balls!

Game

Materials

- Variety of balls

If you had to select just one toy to keep a child entertained, you would do well to select a ball. Both girls and boys like balls, and why wouldn't they? Look at all you can do with them: roll them, throw them, hit them, kick them, balance them, and bounce them. Take your child outside with several balls and just spend an hour or two running around the yard and playing with them.

Clothesline Streamers

Materials

- Different-colored streamers

Take a cord and run it from one tree to another. Next, tie brightly-colored streamers on the cord. When the wind blows, sit and watch the colorful clothesline streamers blow. The streamers will dance in the wind and baby will clap with delight.

Stickball

Materials

- Soft foam ball
- String
- Stick

Game

Since your baby is just beginning to develop coordination, try this game. Tie a ball to a nylon cord, and tie the other end to the stick. Insert the pole in the ground at your baby's level. Show him how to hit the ball. Run around the pole and take turns hitting the ball.

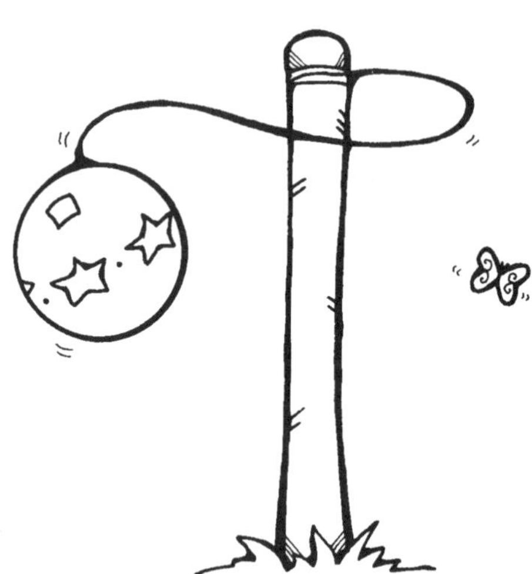

Bounce

Materials

- Large, lightweight towel or small tablecloth
- Small, colorful balls

Game

Let your baby hold one end of the towel while you hold the other one. Put the small balls in the center of the towel. First, roll them around in the towel to get baby accustomed to the activity. Then make a couple of sudden upward movements with your hands and watch the balls dance around the towel. Don't worry if some bounce out, baby will love scrambling around to collect them.

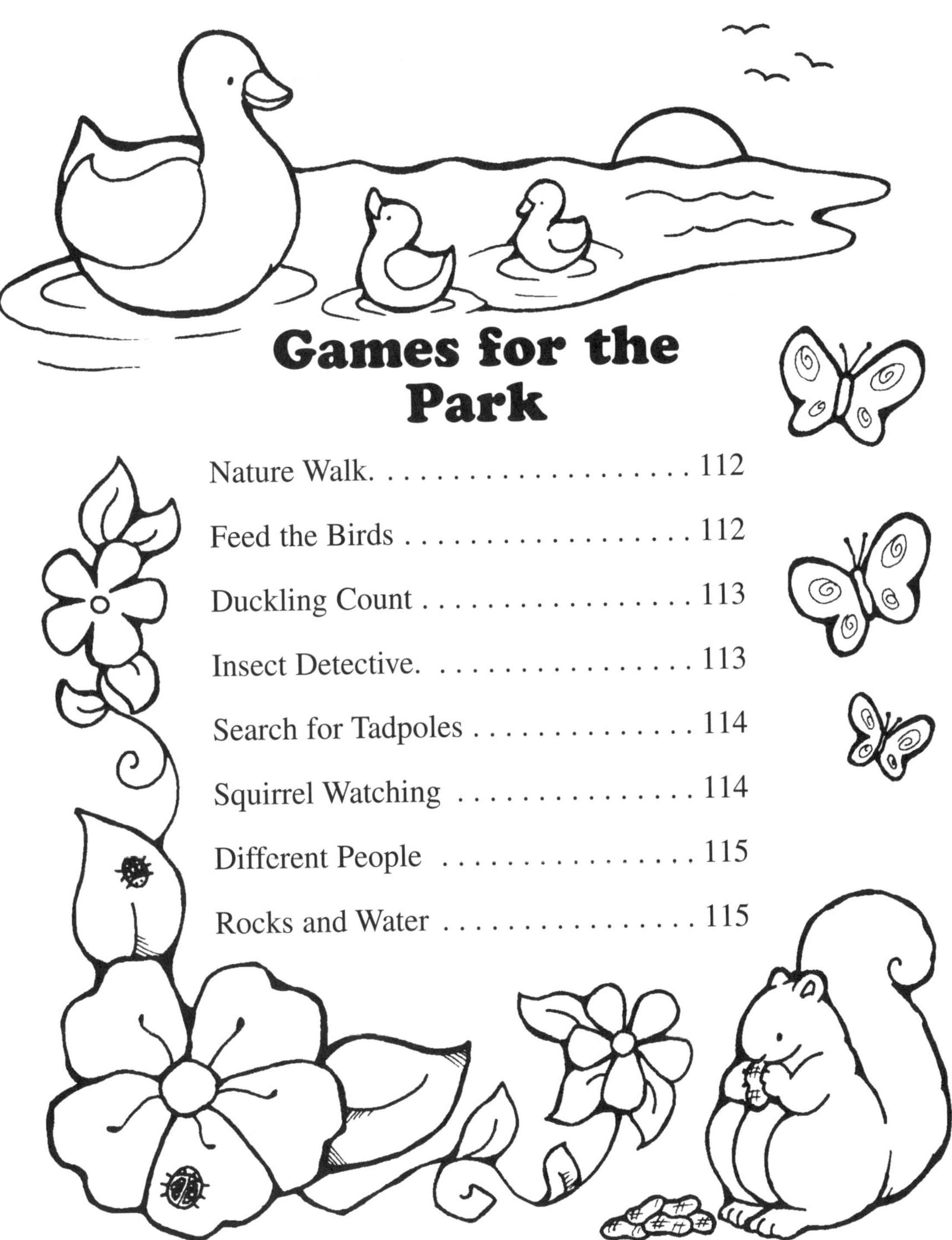

Games for the Park

Nature Walk

Materials

- None

Game

Get off the beaten path! Find a simple nature trail. Colleges and parks are good places to begin the search. Take your baby down the trail. Talk to her about the wildflowers, butterflies, and birds. Who knows, you may even get to see a deer!

Feed the Birds

Materials

- Bread

Game

Feeding the birds has become a tradition in many parts of the country. Save a few crumbs from lunch and let your baby scatter them for the birds. She will love watching the birds gobble up the goodies. While you stand and watch them, pick out your favorite birds and name them.

Duckling Count

Materials

- None

Game

When you are strolling around the park on a beautiful spring day, don't be content simply to look at all those glorious flowers. Also notice all the new life around you! Your baby's favorite animal may be the little ducklings that are scurrying across the pond in pursuit of a busy mother. Stop and watch them. Count each little fuzzy head and count them again when you return—which you are sure to do during such beautiful weather. Talk to your baby about how the ducklings are changing each time you return. Sometimes they hide along the bank. Make a game out of finding them. Neither spring nor ducklings last for long, so enjoy them while you can.

Insect Detective

Materials

- Bug jar
- Insect pictures
- Magnifier

Game

Not all insects bite and sting. Some insects are really fun to have around. Begin this game at home. Get out a picture of the insect of the day. It may be a butterfly, a grasshopper, a ladybug, or even an ant. When you go into the park, both of you become detectives, trying to find the insect of the day. The next time you go to the park, you may use the same insect or change to a new one.

Search for Tadpoles

Game

Materials

- Container
- Pond
- Pond water
- Tadpoles

There is magic at the edge of the pond! Tiny tadpoles dart back and forth. Take your baby and let her see the tadpoles. Let her help you capture a couple of tadpoles in a jar with pond water. Keep the tadpoles in a place where your baby can see them. Watch the amazement on her face as she sees them change from tadpoles into frogs.

Squirrel Watching

Game

Materials

- Squirrels

Sit on the park bench with your baby and watch the squirrels. They will put on quite a show for you! Watch them eat nuts, scurry up trees, and even chase each other. If you're lucky, you might even see the squirrels bury some nuts for winter.

Different People

Materials

- None

Game

Sometimes it is good to take a break from all the activity and play the people-watching game. Position your child's stroller beside you or put him in your lap. Talk to him about all the people walking around the park. "Look at the little girl." "Look at the baby." Then ask him questions and see if he will answer: "Where is the man on the horse?" "Where is the doggie?"

Rocks and Water

Materials

- Nature path

Game

Take advantage of the natural curiosity children have about rocks. As you walk on a nature trail or around a pond, both of you can pick up unusual rocks. If you find a flat stone you might even try skipping it across a pond or a large mud puddle. Those you decide to keep can be brought home for further inspection and comparisons.

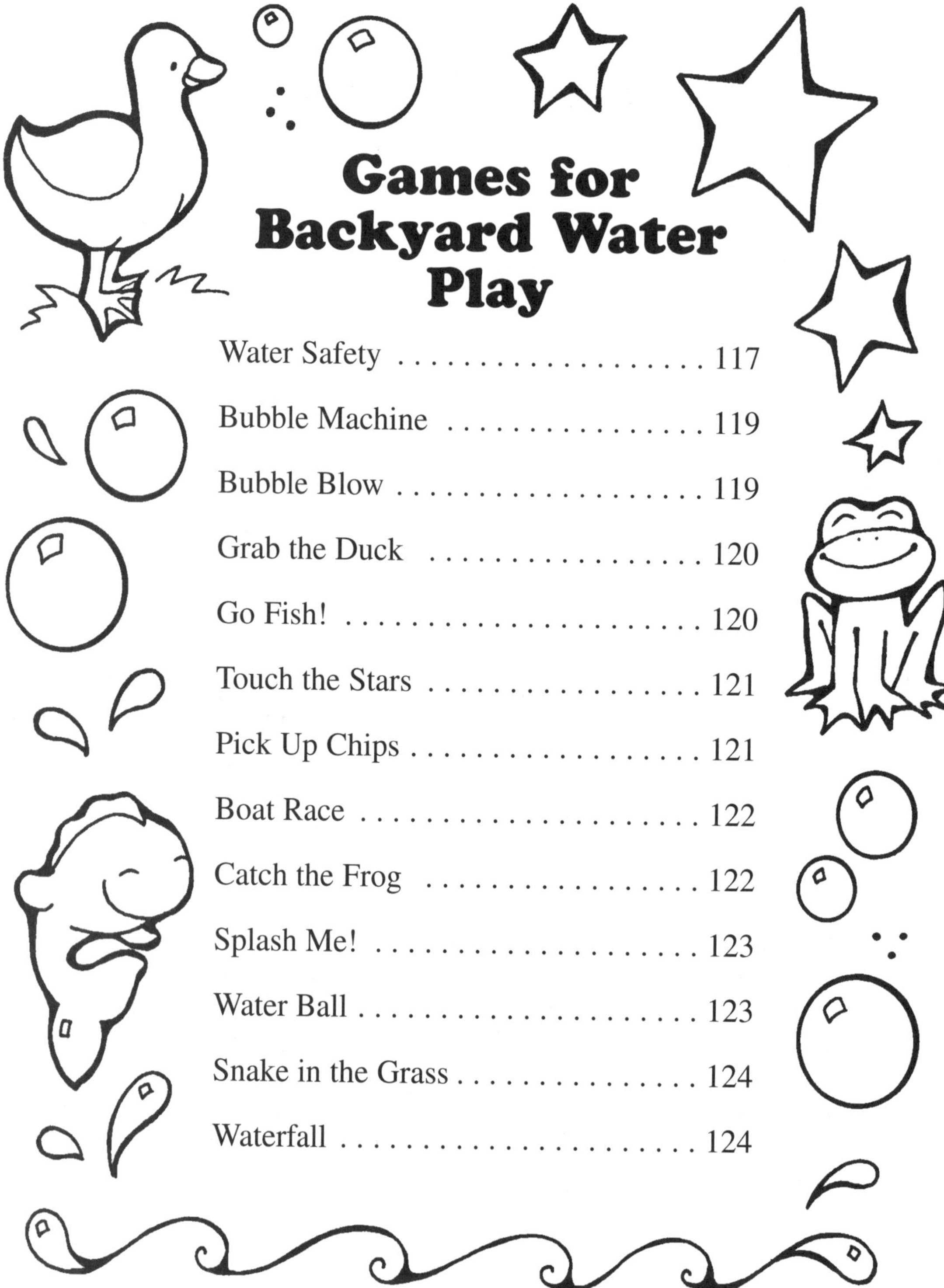

Games for Backyard Water Play

Water Safety

Even if you aren't planning to use the baby pool activities, take a minute to read this page. Water safety is important for everyone. Since young children have a natural attraction to water and want to touch it and play in it, you must be very cautious. The problem with children being around water is that they have no fear, which is probably the reason children ages one to four have the highest drowning rate of any age group in the United States.

What should you do then? Keep your child away from water until he turns four? Not only would that be very difficult since water is all around us—in sinks, bathtubs, toilets, mop buckets, etc.—but you and your baby would miss out on a lot of fun. Also, according to national drowning statistics, it is not usually the child who is being directly supervised in the baby pool who drowns. It is the child who wanders away from his parents for just a few minutes and falls in a neighbor's pool who drowns, or it is the child who is in the bathtub playing while the parent leaves to answer the phone who drowns. Most cases in which young children drown occur when there is a temporary lapse in supervision—five minutes or fewer.

Water Safety *(cont.)*

Can you do anything to keep your child safe from drowning? The good news is there is a lot you can do to help keep your child safe. The following important suggestions should help:

1. Never, not even for a second (drownings occur in seconds, not minutes), leave your young child around water without supervision—not even the mop bucket! (Each year approximately 40 children drown in five-gallon buckets.)
2. Know CPR. Encourage those who supervise your child to know CPR.
3. Don't leave water standing in containers. When you leave the baby pool, empty it and turn it over so it can't collect rain water—even a few inches of water can be dangerous.
4. Survey your immediate neighborhood for trouble spots. Write down the locations of pools, streams, lakes, ponds, etc. Keep the list in an obvious place. If your child is missing, check these spots first.
5. If you have a pool, fence it and lock it. If you have a party and have a pool, make sure someone is responsible for the small children at all times. Don't assume someone is watching them.
6. Don't rely on swimming lessons and water safety devices to keep your child from drowning. They may help, but supervision is the most important step in preventing the drowning of small children.
7. As your child gets to be a toddler and likes to open doors and leave the house, you may want to consider installing new locks or a buzzer or bell system that signals you when a door is open.
8. If you have further questions, call your local Red Cross, fire department, or the National Safety Council at 1-800-621-6244 for more information.

Bubble Machine

Game

Materials

- Batteries
- Bubble machine
- Bubble solution

When baby first gets around water, he may be frightened. Your goal at this age is just to get him used to the water and have fun with him. Try putting a bubble machine on an outdoor table at the far side of the baby pool. Turn it on before you bring him to the pool. He will probably see the bubbles even before he notices the water. Follow him as he moves toward the bubble machine. He will probably want to step in the pool to get to the bubble machine. If he does, help him in the pool and step in the pool with him. Chase the bubbles with him and let him pop the bubbles when they land on the water. He probably will want to get into the pool, but let him decide for himself. Be there to support him, but don't force him to get into the pool before he is ready. He may spend time around the edge playing, or he may be more prone to get into the pool if there are other children around.

Bubble Blow

Game

Materials

- Bubble solution

Once he is in the pool and feels comfortable enough to sit down, let him blow bubbles. Take the bubbles to the edge of the baby pool. Sit on the ground beside him and blow bubbles into the pool. Let him take turns trying to blow bubbles that will land in the water.

Grab the Duck

Materials

- Plastic floating ducks or other animals

Game

Grab the Duck is good game for a baby getting comfortable with the water. Take plastic floating ducks or other plastic floating animals and throw them in the water. Help her in the water and be her cheerleader as she tries to grab the animals and put them back on the outside of the pool. When she has collected all the ducks, don't be surprised if she throws them back in for another game.

Go Fish!

Materials

- Plastic fish (They should not float.)

Game

When your baby is sitting in the water and enjoying herself, throw colorful plastic fish into the water. Make sure that they don't float. Place some fish near her and some a little farther away. Tell her to go fishing. The ones closer to her will be easy to reach. The ones farther away will cause her to reach and put more of her upper body in the water. You may even want to take turns with her. Kneel on the outside of the pool. Lean over and grab a fish. Then let her have a turn.

Touch the Stars

Materials

- Different-colored metallic stars
- Water

Game

Let your baby pick out his favorite colored metallic stars. Stick them on his toes. When he sits down in the water, ask him to touch his stars. If he does it correctly, most of his upper body will get wet.

Pick Up Chips

Materials

- Poker chips or plastic coasters
- Water

Game

Children like this game, especially if they get to play with the chips. Drop the chips in the pool around your baby after he sits down. Tell him to gather the chips. As he reaches for them, he should get some of his upper body wet. As he picks up each chip, have him hand it to you. Don't let him have enough time to put the chips in his mouth. After you get out of the pool and get dried off, take turns sorting and stacking the treasure chips.

Boat Race

Materials

- Two safe lightweight plastic boats

Game

When baby gets comfortable in the pool, play this game with her. Put two very lightweight plastic boats in the water. Get on your knees beside the baby pool. Put one of the boats in front of you in the water. Lean over and blow bubbles in the water, directly behind the little boat. The bubbles will make the boat move. Put the other boat in front of baby. Let her try to blow bubbles. When she learns how to move the boat, see who can blow a boat the farthest distance. If another child is in the pool with her, let them race their boats across the pool. Before letting your child play with the boat, make sure it is age-appropriate and doesn't have any small pieces that could be swallowed.

Catch the Frog

Materials

- Safe wind-up water toy

Game

Wind-up water toys are always fun and inexpensive toys to use in a baby pool. They come in a variety of shapes, sizes, and colors, and you can find almost any type of water animal you desire. The frog is a favorite because it makes children laugh as it moves through the water. You don't have to use a frog though. You may prefer a dolphin or a whale. Just wind the animal up and drop it in the water. It will automatically start swimming across the pool. When you put it in the water, say, "There goes the frog! Catch it!" As always, check the toy before you buy it to make sure it is safe for your baby. Don't select a toy that has small pieces that could be swallowed.

Splash Me!

Game

Materials

- None

On one of those warm days when you want to get wet too, play "Splash Me!" Position yourself anywhere you wish around the baby pool. You can either stand up or get on your hands and knees. Lean over the pool and say, "Look at me splash!" Splash water in the pool, being careful not to wet your baby. You don't want to frighten him. Ask him, "Can you splash, too?" He will probably delight in this activity. When he gets to be a strong "splasher," say, "I bet you can't splash me!" When he splashes you, make a funny noise and say, "You got me!" Move to another spot around the pool and say, "Bet you can't splash me again!" Continue the game until you are both cooled off.

Water Ball

Game

Materials

- Small, inflatable beach ball

Beach balls are favorites among children because they are light and easy to handle. Get a small beach ball, blow it up, and take it out to the baby pool for hours of fun. Once your baby is sitting in the water, kneel down beside him and push the ball to him. He will have a great time getting the ball and pushing it back to you. When he tires of that game, try tossing the ball back and forth. If the ball deflates, don't let baby play with it.

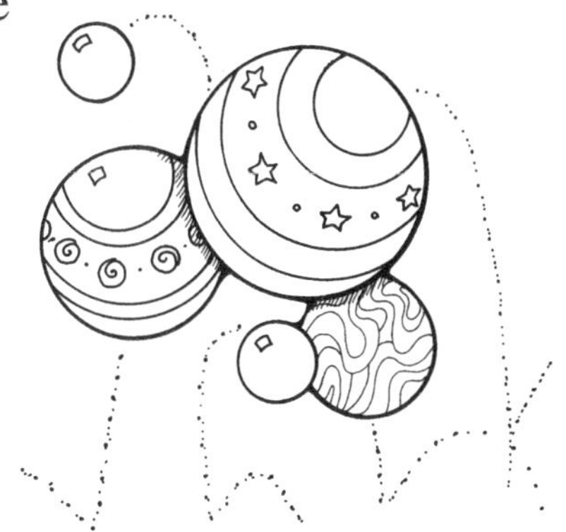

Snake in the Grass

Materials

- Water hose
- Water hose spray attachment

Game

Want to hear squeals of delight? Surprise your baby with this game. On a hot summer afternoon, you and baby go out in the yard in your swimsuits. Attach the sprayer to the water hose. Turn the hose on and yell, "Snake in the Grass. He is going to get you!" Chase your baby, making a hissing sound, and spraying him gently with the hose. Don't forget to let him have a turn. (Of course, you're safe until he learns how to work the sprayer.)

Waterfall

Materials

- Camera (optional)
- Sprinkler or water hose attachments

Game

If you want a game that will last for hours, this is the one! Turn on a sprinkler or bury the hose attachment in the ground so that the water shoots out of the ground and arches into a waterfall. Turn the hose on and chase your baby through the waterfall, let her ride her truck through the waterfall, or let her chase other children through the waterfall; the games are endless, and the pictures from these adventures will entertain your family for years to come.

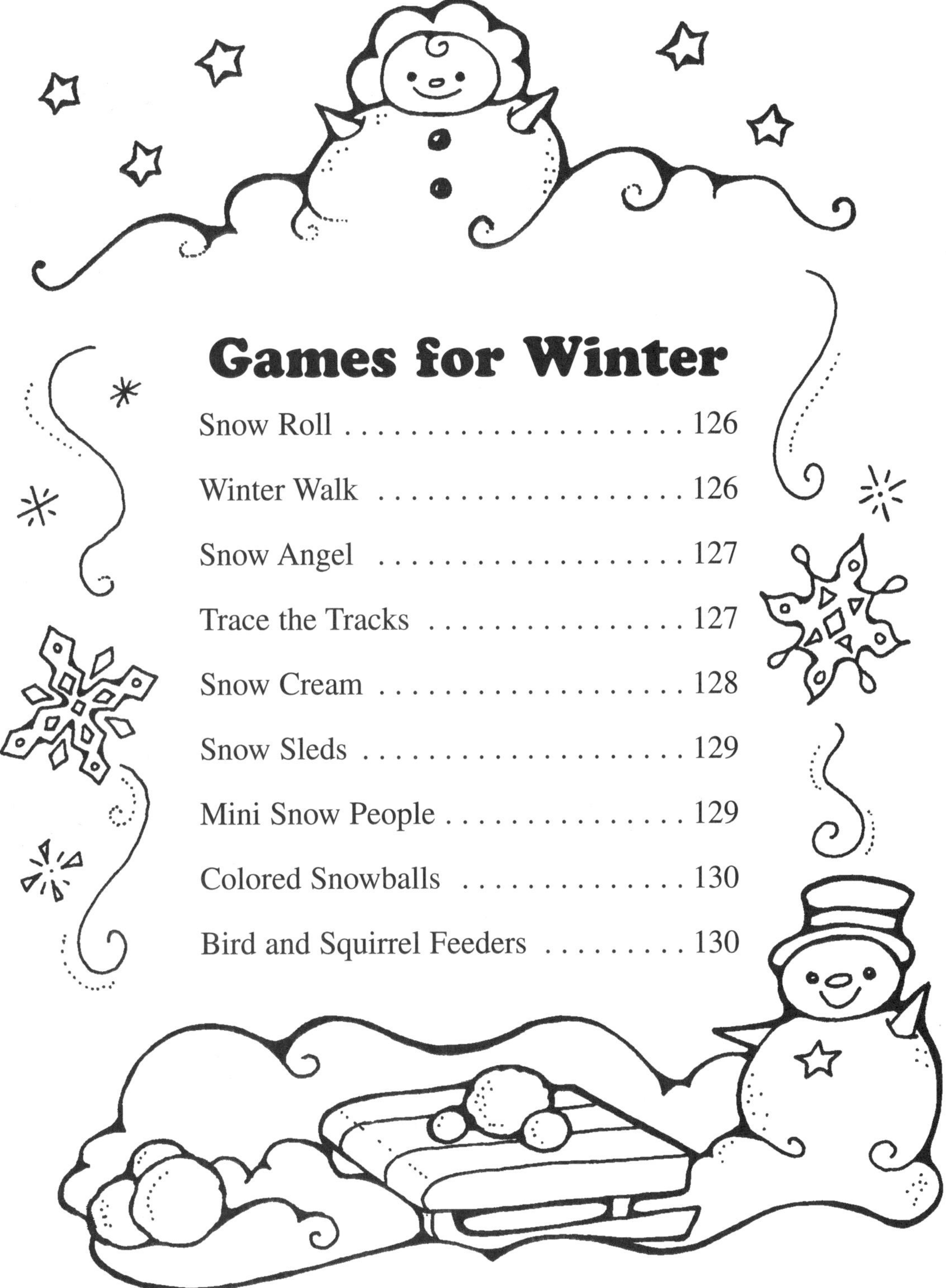

Games for Winter

Snow Roll

Game

Materials

- Snow
- Warm, waterproof clothes

Baby's first snow outing is always an exciting time! Make it a special for her and you. Zip baby up in warm waterproof clothing, hat, scarf, and gloves or mittens. If you and your baby are dressed to get really wet, go to the top of a small hill. Lie down on your back. Roll down the hill. See who gets to the bottom first!

Winter Walk

Game

Materials

- Warm clothes
- Snow

The magic of snow is that it changes how our world looks. Take your baby for a walk around the yard or even the block. Tell him what the objects were before they were covered with snow. You may not be able to name everything at first glance. Try to spot dripping icicles or frosty windowpanes to view.

Snow Angel

Materials

- None

Game

Go out to the middle of the yard where the clean, fresh snow is, and lie down. Spread your arms out and move them up and down. At the same time, move your legs in and out. Get your baby to do the same. Soon you will have a family of snow angels and be ready for hot cocoa and cookies.

Trace the Tracks

Materials

- Big ball

Game

Be sleuths in the snow. Go out a few minutes before you take your baby out. Make big steps in the snow. Make a couple of twists and turns right behind a bush or tree and hide the big ball. When you go back to the house, be careful not to disturb the trail. Tell your baby you are going to go on a hunt for the big ball. Tell him he has to follow the footprints to find it. Follow behind him, helping him through the snow. Watch his surprise when he finds the big ball.

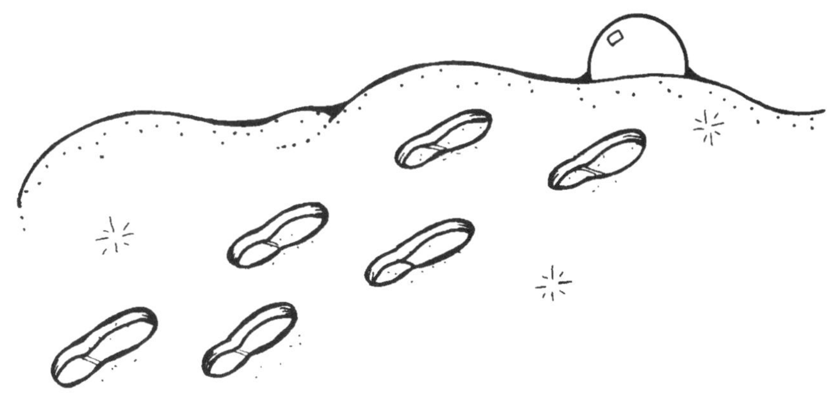

Snow Cream

Game

Materials

- Snow or crushed ice
- Sugar
- Vanilla extract or Maple syrup

If you live in an area where there isn't much pollution, you may want to try a small bowl of snow cream. You and your baby should collect a small bowl of snow. Put in a couple of drops of maple syrup or vanilla extract and sugar to taste. Then sit and enjoy your free ice cream. If you don't have access to snow, try this with crushed ice and pretend you are in the snow.

Snow Sleds

Materials

- Snow sled

Game

Pick a very small hill for this age group. Climb on the snow sled and put your baby on, too. Take one big push, and there you go! Mark the finishes in the snow and see which time you went the farthest.

Mini Snow People

Materials

- Snow
- Raisins
- Bite-size carrots
- Cabbage leaves
- Toothpicks

Game

Big snow people are too large for little people to handle. Sit on the step and make a family of mini snow people. Roll three small balls per person. Use toothpicks for the arms, raisins for the eyes and mouths, and miniature carrots for the noses. Top them off by using cabbage leaves for their hair. As the snow melts, ants or birds will enjoy eating the raisins, and bunnies will enjoy the carrots and cabbage leaves. If you don't live in a rural area, you may want to throw the leftovers in your compost pile.

Colored Snowballs

Materials

- Bowls
- Food coloring
- Snow

Game

Colored snowballs help your baby learn his colors while you play. Bring food coloring and bowls outside. Let your baby get a big handful of snow and drop it in a bowl. Put drops of food coloring in the bowl and let him work it in with his hands. While he is mixing say, "Look at that blue snow." Show him how to form a ball with the snow. Then move out of the way as he throws it!

Bird and Squirrel Feeders

Materials

- Bird and squirrel feeders
- Bird and squirrel food

Game

While the snow is on the ground, feeders are good for the animals. They also provide wonderful warm entertainment for your family. Snug inside the house, you and your baby can watch as the animals take turns at the feeders. While you eat cookies and milk, talk about the different birds and count the squirrels. What an enjoyable warm game on a cold day!

Games for the Beach

Sand Cities

Game

Materials

- Bucket
- Plastic cars and people
- Sand
- Shovels
- Water

Ever get tired of making sand castles? Play the Sand Cities game, instead. This game is especially wonderful for extended family vacations at the beach because all the kids can play. Make sure you have a lot of room around you and your group. Draw a large circle in the sand and tell everyone that is where the city is. They are not to go out of the circle. Make sure the youngest have shovels and let them dig. Tell the other kids that they are in charge of making the buildings and secret tunnels that connect the buildings together. When they get tired of building, dump the plastic men and cars in the middle of the city and watch their faces light up. Make sure you have enough cars for everyone because all the children will enjoy rolling and racing cars down the city streets.

If you and your baby are the only two at the beach, the game can still be a lot of fun. Just make the circle small and let simple mounds of sand be your buildings. Your baby will enjoy rolling the plastic cars around the mounds of sand.

Shell Angels

Materials

- Crayons
- Cut outs
- Glue
- Safety scissors
- Shells
- Two collectors' bags

Game

Collecting shells is always a favorite pastime at the beach, and it is a wonderful way to teach your baby shapes and sizes. Add a little more fun to this activity by making the shells into game pieces. Begin by cutting out heads, arms, and feet. If older kids are around, they may want to do the cutting. Then take a nice long walk with your child or children and begin collecting shells. To encourage sorting skills, ask your child to put little shells in one bag and big shells in another bag.

When you get back from your walk, spread the big shells on the table. Select only the shells that are fan shaped. Put the rest back in the bag. Ask your baby to find the angel's head. When he points to it, pick it up and glue it on the point of the shell. Ask him where an arm is and continue the game until all the parts are on the angel. Collecting shells has turned into a fun body parts game, and everyone gets an angel to use as a decoration for the holidays.

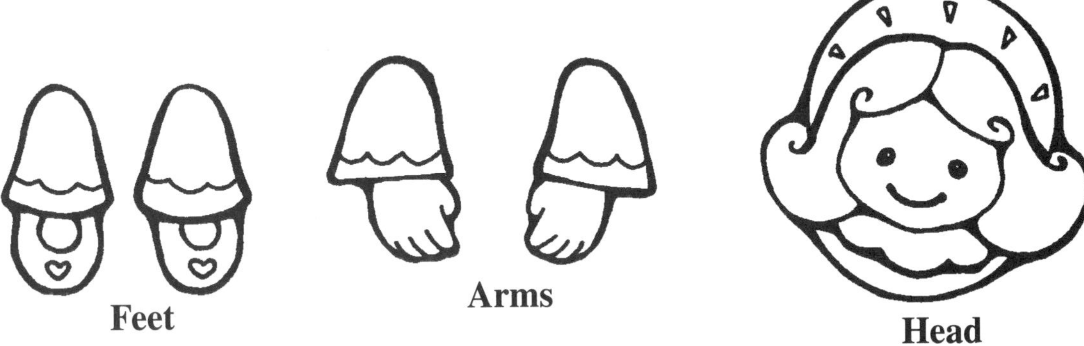

Birds on the Pier

Game

Materials

- None

Piers are rich environments for young children. Fishermen often line the rails, hoping for that great catch. Birds often perch on the wooden poles, hoping for the great catch that got away. Take your little one for a walk out on the pier. Be very careful that she holds your hand so she won't get away from you and fall in. Sit on a bench, hold her in your lap, and when you see a bird land on the pier, whisper in her ear, "Bird on the pier." After you have repeated this activity several times, point to the birds and listen to see if she mimics you. After she mimics you several times, change the word "bird" to the name of the bird, "Seagull on the pier." Soon she will begin to name her birds.

Big Fish, Little Fish

Game

Materials

- None

Many beaches have aquariums. Take your child to one of the big tanks that has a variety of fish. When a big fish passes by say, "Big fish," using a deep voice. When a little fish passes by say "Little fish," using a small, squeaky voice. Then when the next fish goes by, say, "Big fish?" and wait for her reply. If she says "No," say, "Little fish?" Repeat the activity. Don't be surprised if one day in the middle of a pet store or watching a nature show, she screams, "Big fish!"

Fishy Feet

Materials

- None

Game

If you are by a lake or pond, you might see tiny fish swimming in schools around your feet. As you and your baby wade, watch for these little fish. When you see them say, "Stand still. Fishy feet." When the fish dart off, yell, "Go get them." Run for a short distance in the direction the fish swam.

Sand Dollars

Materials

- Sand dollars

Game

Sand dollars are truly one of the treasures of the sea. Older children love to spend hours diving for these creatures. Younger children are fascinated by the way they look and feel. Begin this game by collecting or letting older children collect three or four sand dollars. Place them near the edge of the shore and encourage your little one to reach down and find them. Some children may refuse to touch them because of the strange texture, but other children will love the game. Of course, it is always preferable to leave nature the way you found it, so you want to put the sand dollars back in their sandy homes after you play with them.

Disappearing Feet

Game

Materials

- Water
- Sand
- Waves

As the tide comes in, talk a walk along the edge of the beach with your baby. Come back exactly the same way and show him how the waves have wiped away his foot prints.

Sand Drawing

Game

Materials

- Stick
- Wet sand

Go to the edge of the beach with your child. Smooth the sand with your hand. Find two sticks and take turns scribbling in the sand. When the area is full of scribbles, smooth out the sand and start again.

Frisbee Toss

Materials

- Frisbee

Game

The beach is a wonderful place for a Frisbee Toss. Most children, regardless of age, seem to love tossing and catching these colorful discs of plastic. Modify the game for your young child. Have him stand in front of you facing away from you. Toss the Frisbee lightly in the air and encourage him to run after the Frisbee while you run after him. One day he may surprise you by picking up the Frisbee and throwing it back.

Popping Balls

Materials

- Sand
- Brightly-colored balls

Game

Take three brightly-colored balls. Then hide them in the sand. Ask your baby to find them. After he repeats the activity several times, take him to the edge of the shore and hide the balls under the water in the sand. Ask your baby to find them. Watch his surprised look when, after digging just a little, the balls pop up to the surface.

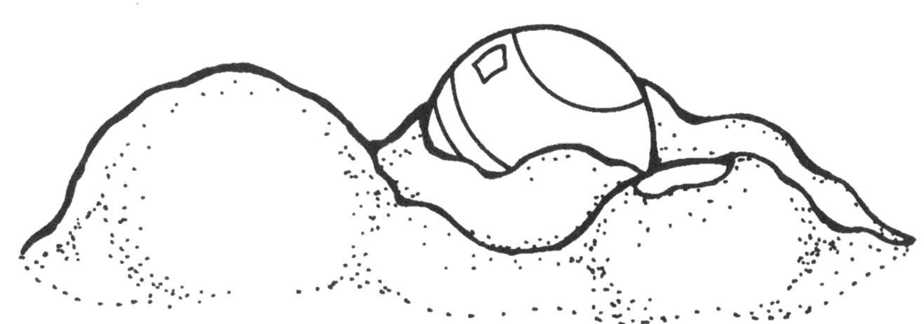

Games for the Garden

Simple Tools

Game

Materials

- Children's garden tools: spade, trowel, shovel, basket, gloves*

To make your little one feel like a real gardener, give him a set of his own tools. Make a game out of getting the tools out of the basket, by asking, "Where is the spade? Where is the trowel? Where are your gloves?" Take him outside and demonstrate how each tool works by using yours. Soon he will be imitating you.

** Very small gloves can sometimes be found in gardening supply stores or catalogs.*

Mountain Royalty

Game

Materials

- Mound of dirt
- Crown of honeysickle
- Stick scepter

Take a break from garden work and play king or queen of the mountain with your baby. To encourage climbing, find a mound of dirt and climb with him to the top. When he reaches the very top, crown him with the honeysuckle crown and give him the stick scepter. Take the stick and tell him you will catch him as he runs down the mound. Of course, he may want to keep his crown, even when he is no longer royalty.

Bean Tent

Materials

- Six poles
- Climbing bean plants

Game

Create a cool, hidey-hole for the garden. Take six poles of equal length and tie the tops together. Spread out the legs and plant them firmly in the ground. Plant a climbing bean plant at the base of each pole. Water the plants and watch them grow. In no time, you and your baby will have a tent to crawl into. It is a wonderful place to have a midday tea party. When you are finished, stay in the shade of the tent and pick the beans for your evening meal.

Butterfly Chase

Game

Materials

- None

Babies love to touch and explore everything. To show her what a butterfly feels and looks like, go on a butterfly chase. Begin by letting her run after the butterflies. Although she probably won't catch one, she'll have fun trying. When she is tired, sit very still and maybe you will get lucky enough to have a butterfly land by you just long enough to let her take a look at it. Butterflies are fun to watch as they go from flower to flower gathering nectar.

Butterfly Garden

Game

Materials

- Flowers or other plants with sweet herb-like scents and brilliant colors.*
- Gloves
- Spade

Begin the spring by growing a butterfly garden for you and your baby. Butterflies love colorful, sweet flowers. Begin the activity by taking your baby to a plant nursery. Let her walk around and look at all the different types of plants. Talk to her about the colors and categories: trees, shrubs, flowers. Select a few plants for your butterfly garden. When you get home, get a spade, some work gloves, and the plants and take them to the area you have selected in your yard. Let your baby play with the gloves and let her dig. Then place the plants in the ground and let her pat the dirt around the plants. Soon you will have colorful butterflies flitting around the yard.

**Butterflies are attracted to many flowers including impatiens, zinnias, and nasturtiums. Some nurseries offer "Butterfly Garden" seed packets and kits.*

Spider Web

Game

Materials

- None

Spider webs are fascinating pieces of nature's art. Take your baby outside just after a heavy dew or rainfall. Hold him up to the web and let him see the wonderful patterns. Make a game out of finding the spider. When he finds the spider, gently touch the web and let him watch the spider scurry. Say, "Look! Mr. Spider thinks he caught a big fly." Let him create his own spider web by wrapping white string between two chairs. Let him stand on one side of the web while you stand on the other. Take turns playing spider and fly. One of you sticks your hand through the web. The other one tries to grab the hand before it gets away.

Bird's Nest

Game

Materials

- Bowl
- Plastic eggs
- Straw or grass
- Toy birds

In early spring, you may be lucky enough to find a real bird's nest. Take your baby out to see it every day. Talk to him about the baby birds hatching, growing up, and flying away. Recreate a bird's nest in your kitchen. Take a bowl and get your baby to fill it full of grass and sticks to make the nest. Put the toy birds inside the plastic eggs and ask him where the eggs go. He should put them in the nest. Next, ask him what happens to the eggs. Let him open the eggs and find the birds inside. Finally, ask him what happens to the baby birds when they get bigger. Show him how they fly away.

Fruit Picking

Materials

- Baskets
- Gloves

Game

Blackberries, blueberries, raspberries, and strawberries are all berries kids enjoy picking. Begin by showing your baby how to pick berries, avoiding the thorns and green berries. Also, caution her to stay on the edge of the bushes to avoid creatures that may be resting in the shade on a warm summer day. Make a game as you pick. Say "one, two, three, and one for me." Put three berries in the basket and one in your mouth. (Of course, you should not play this game without washing the fruit if your bushes have been sprayed with insecticide.)

Vegetable Measuring Stick

Materials

- Okra or corn stalk

Game

Okra and corn may be two things that actually grow faster than your baby. A little game to start teaching baby about tall and taller is the okra or corn measuring stick. After you plant your okra or corn and see the first green sprouts coming up, say "Which is taller?" Point to your baby and say, "You are taller!" Every couple of days go out and repeat the activity. The okra or corn will soon be over your baby's head and may even be over your head. At that point the okra or corn may seem gigantic to your baby.

Tomato Toss

Game

Materials

- Bucket
- Overripe tomatoes
- Garden gloves

Usually, around the end of July, you have tomatoes that are attacked by insects or birds or that just don't ripen well. Don't just toss them away. Make a game with them. Collect your rotten tomatoes in a basket. Bring the basket near the compost pile. Help baby toss the tomatoes onto the pile.

Worm Garden

Game

Materials

- Rotten vegetables, fruits, and decayed leaves
- Worms
- Water
- Soil
- Glass jar
- Grease pencil

Another activity you can do with those rotten veggies and fruits is to help your little one set up a worm garden. Mark your jar with a grease pencil at the halfway mark. Tell your baby to fill the jar with the decayed material to that mark. Put enough water in the jar to moisten the mixture. Finally, the exciting part! Let your baby drop the worms into the mixture and watch them go to work. As you observe the worms, play a game of counting and finding all the worms. Your baby may be surprised when there are more and more worms. After the worms multiply, help your baby place them back in the garden so they will enrich your soil for next year.

Sour Face Game

Materials

- Deviled egg tray or any tray with sections
- Variety of cooked fresh fruits and vegetables

Game

Once your baby has begun eating vegetables, put small samples of cooked veggies and fruits in the tray compartments. Let baby sample each one and see which fruits and vegetables he automatically likes and which ones he doesn't like. His sour face will be your first clue! After playing this game, you will have a good idea of which foods have to be introduced several more times before he has a chance to acquire a taste for them. Usually, it takes a baby at least 15 times tasting a new food before he will enjoy it. Of course, some foods may never appeal to him, but introduce them several more times before you give up.

Scarecrow Face Game

Materials

- Felt eyes, nose, and mouth
- Hat
- Yarn

Game

Another fun body parts game is Scarecrow Face. If other kids are around, you may want them to make the body of the scarecrow, or you can make the body by stuffing blue jeans and a flannel shirt with old towels, newspapers or pillow stuffing. Make the face out of an old pillowcase, stuff it with whatever you used in the body, and tie it at the bottom with a heavy rope or string. Then let your baby help you make the scarecrow face. Put glue on the back of felt pieces and let baby place them on the scarecrow's face.

Sorting Veggies

Game

Materials

- corn
- Okra
- Potatoes
- Tomatoes

You can use any garden vegetables to play this game, but you may want to start with okra, potatoes, corn, and tomatoes because they are very different in shape, size, and color. When you come in from the garden, dump the veggies out on the kitchen table and get your baby to help you sort them into three piles. As your baby masters these veggies, you may want to change to game to make it harder by getting vegetables that look more alike.

Vegetable Matching Game

Game

Materials

- Glue sticks
- Gardening magazines, and seed catalogs
- Precut vegetables
- Small brown paper sacks
- Wooden stakes

Cut out pictures of vegetables that you have in your garden. Count out enough small brown sacks to have one for each vegetable. When you have finished, let your baby come in and help. Help him glue vegetable pictures onto the brown bags. Place them over the stakes and go out to the garden. See how many stakes he can match with the correct vegetables.

Nature Rubbings

Game

Want to add a new touch to scribbling? Make your child's scribbles into nature rubbings. After one of your walks, take your collection of flowers and leaves and lay them out on the table. Pick out your favorites. Put them between two pieces of paper and press them under a heavy book or between the pages. In a few days, take out the pressed flowers and leaves. Lay them on the table and put a piece of paper over them. Help your child make the rubbing by holding the paper steady and both of you pressing down on the crayon while you scribble together. Images of the leaves and flowers should start appearing on the paper. Your child will think it is magic, and you will have pretty rubbings for new refrigerator displays, or you may want to frame them.

Materials

- Crayons
- Paper
- Pressed flowers
- Pressed leaves

Magic Flowers

Game

On one of your walks, collect a few pieces of Queen Anne's lace. If this weed is not indigenous to your area, select any flower or weed that is primarily white. Queen Anne's lace is especially nice because of its delicate patterns. Cut the stems at a slant. When you get home, let your baby put the flowers in three separate vases or glasses filled with water. Allow her to watch as you put different-colored drops of food coloring in each vase. Your baby will be surprised when the white flowers turn red, yellow, and blue in a day or two.

Materials

- Food coloring
- Queen Anne's lace or other white flower or weed
- Vases

Ants

Materials

- Ant hill

Game

If you can't stand the thoughts of a broken ant farm all over the bedroom floor, take advantage of the natural ant farms in and around your garden. Usually, they are somewhere nearby because they like the tilled soil. Sit down with your baby and watch the ants move around, carrying objects much bigger than they are. Talk to your baby about how hard they work. Just be careful he doesn't sit or play in the ant bed!

Chrysalis

Materials

- Chrysalis
- Container

Game

Usually, if you look hard in the springtime, you can find at least one chrysalis in your garden. Talk to baby about how a caterpillar turns into a butterfly. Check the chrysalis daily and let him observe some more of nature's magic. If you want to encourage butterflies to live in your garden, you may want to check your nature store or garden center for butterfly houses or the materials to start a butterfly garden. (See page 141 for more suggestions.)

Carrot Pull

Materials

- Baskets
- Carrots
- Gloves

Game

When carrots get green and bushy on top, take baby out to help harvest. Put gloves on her and take her out to the garden. Say, "I wonder what's hiding in the dirt? Do you want to see?" When she says, "Yes," let her pull up the carrot. Say, "Look, it's a carrot! And we grew it." Let her repeat the activity a few times.

Potato Dig

Materials

- Basket
- Gloves
- Potatoes

Game

Potatoes are fun to dig because you never know how many there are or what size they are while they're hiding under the earth. Treat a potato dig like an Easter egg hunt. When the tops of the potatoes die, it is time to dig them. Take your baby with her basket and gloves outside. Shovel most of the dirt away. Let her begin digging with a spade or even her hands. She will be excited when she begins finding the potatoes. See who has the most potatoes in his or her basket at the end of the dig.

Leaf Piles

Game

Materials

- Rakes

Fall is a time for preparing the soil and the garden for next year's crop. Make it a happy time with your child. If you have any hardwood trees around, chances are you need to do a little raking to clean up your garden. Get your baby a little plastic rake. You take the big metal one and make a heaping big pile of leaves. Surprise your baby by jumping right in the middle of the pile. He will soon join you. After a few minutes of play and throwing leaves on each other, hop out of the pile, get your rakes, and rake them up again. Or get the lawn mower with the leaf bag and clean up your mess in minutes. Empty the bag and you've got a great mulch.

Drying Flowers

Game

Materials

- Flowers
- Nail
- String

Getting baby to help you is fun for him and for you. Get your baby to help you collect the last summer blooms in your garden. Add a few herbs to the collection. Get a string and tie the flowers and herbs together by the stems. Hang them upside down and let them dry. After they have dried and you have made pretty arrangements with them for the winter months, be sure to tell baby that these are the flowers he picked.

Vegetable Stationery

Materials

- Fingerpaint
- Paper
- Potatoes, cucumbers, celery, corn, squash
- Sharp knife

Game

If you and your baby are good gardeners, you may have more vegetables than you can possibly eat. When you get tired of canning and freezing, play this game. Cut a potato, cucumber, and squash in half. Put them face down on a plastic or paper plate. Place corn and celery whole on the plate. Get out different-colored finger paints and squeeze a little of each color on a plate. Put a large piece of white paper in front of you and your baby and start making vegetable paintings. Use the cucumbers, potatoes, and squash like stamps. Dip them in the paint and stamp them on the paper. Roll the other veggies in paint and roll them on the paper. Let your paintings dry. Fold them in half to use them as summer stationery.

Gift Baskets

Materials

- Baskets
- Brightly-colored ribbon
- Vegetables
- Vegetable Stationery

Game

A rewarding way to make use of extra veggies is to make gift baskets. Put all the baskets on the table. Play a game with your baby while filling the baskets. "You put in a carrot, and I'll put in a potato," etc. Then write a quick note on your vegetable stationery and attach it to the basket with brightly-colored ribbon. Your baby will have fun playing and also learn about giving.

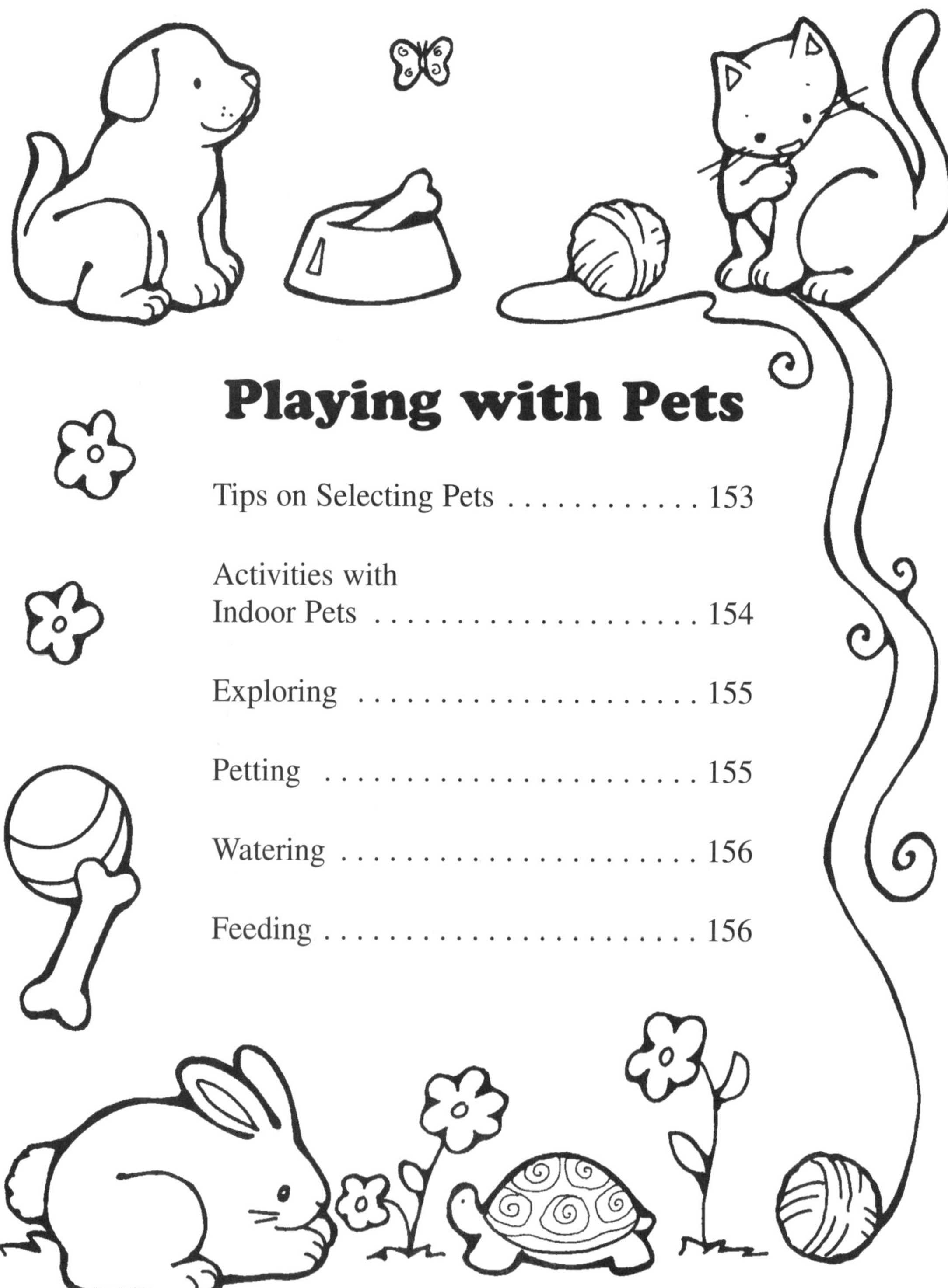

Playing with Pets

Tips on Selecting Pets

Many people believe that pets and children naturally go together. Unfortunately, that belief is not necessarily true. First of all, your children may be allergic to their pets. Many children suffer from cat and dog allergies and are heartbroken when they have to give up their furry friends. Before you get a pet, find others who have them. Let your child spend time around other animals before you make an addition to your home.

The second cause of concern is that your small child may be afraid of his pet. He may enjoy it for a few weeks until it gets big enough to scratch him or knock him down. For example, Labrador retrievers are wonderful family dogs but not necessarily for tiny children. The average Lab grows to between 70 and 80 pounds. An 18-month old is easily upset by a six-week-old Lab puppy. After the movie *101 Dalmatians*, the animal shelters were filled with Dalmatian puppies. Dalmatians, although attractive puppies and dogs, are usually hyperactive and can be hard to manage. To avoid these mistakes, take your child to a pet store or veterinarian and ask for advice. Many pet stores now have computers that will help match your family with the perfect pet.

Finally, care of pets is a consideration. Most dogs like a lot of attention. Some need to be brushed or clipped on a regular basis. This not only takes a lot of time, but is expensive. Cats are much less expensive but may not have the temperaments for small children. Again, do a little investigative work before falling for those cute faces.

Activities with Indoor Pets

If you have indoor pets, they can provide hours of fun for you and your baby. Your baby will learn a lot, too, simply by watching them and playing with them.

Gerbils: You and baby can spend time watching gerbils everyday, especially if they have a litter of babies. Gerbils are also interesting to watch as they drink water or run on their exercise wheel.

Birds: Baby will be delighted to watch your pet bird fly. If you have one that speaks, he and baby can learn a few words by talking to each other. Some birds also make beautiful music, if you don't mind the constant noise.

Dogs and Cats: You and baby can take turns holding dogs and cats. You can have fun playing a game of tug-of-war with a puppy and a sock or an entertaining game of keep away with a kitten and a tiny ball of yarn. Puppies enjoy fetching balls. Kittens enjoy chasing almost anything. Both of these animals can provide hours of fun, and eventually, they will feel like part of the family.

Fish: Fish come in such a variety of colors, shapes, sizes, and types that they are always fun to watch. Set up a fresh or saltwater aquarium. Just make sure it is out of baby's reach. You won't have to worry about forgetting to feed the fish. Baby will beg you to let him do it.

Exploring

Materials

- Pet

Babies explore pets just like everything else. If you're not careful, they will pull their ears, put their fingers in their eyes, and pull their tails. Some pets have a lot of patience and allow this exploration, while others will bite, scratch, or scare baby. To avoid this situation, explore the pet with your baby. Talk about the pet's eyes, tail, feathers, ears, etc. Show her how to handle the animal without frightening it or hurting it.

Petting

Materials

- Pet

Babies don't naturally know how to treat a pet. Learning how to treat a pet is not only fun but necessary for the safety of your baby and your pet. Take your new pet out into the yard or out of the cage and show baby how to hold and pet the animal. Explain to baby that it is best to pet an animal from its head to its tail. Encourage baby to practice gently petting his own head. Emphasize the need to be careful and gentle at all times. Let him try to imitate you. You may have to repeat the activity several times, but you should have a great time doing it!

Watering

Materials

- Water container
- Hose or faucet

If your family has a pet, teaching your child how to care for it is important. Begin by letting her put water in your pet's water container. If it is an outside dog, baby should enjoy using the water hose. If it is an inside pet, like a gerbil, baby should enjoy seeing the water rise to the top of the container.

Feeding

Materials

- Measuring cup

When your baby is beginning to enjoy pouring, let her fill a measuring cup with food and pour it in your pet's bowl or container. She will not only enjoy pouring and helping, but she will begin exploring the concept of measurement.

Resources

Books

Beall, Pamela C., and Nipp, Susan Hagen. ***Wee Sing for Babies.*** Putnam Publ. Grp.,1996

Beebe, Brooke McKamy. ***Best Bets for Babies.*** Delta Books, 1993.

Healy, Jane M. ***Your Child's Growing Mind.*** Doubleday, 1994.

Herd, Meg. ***Learn and Play in the Garden.*** Barron's Educational Service, Inc., 1997.

Kleiner, Lynn. ***Kids Make Music, Babies Make Music, Too!*** Warner Brothers, 1998.

Montroll, John. ***Origami Sculptures.*** Dover, 1991.

Shelov, Steven P. ***Caring for Your Baby and Young Child.*** Bantam Books, 1998.

White, Burton L. ***The New First Three Years of Life.*** Fireside, 1995.

Web Sites for Parents

If you want to talk to other parents from your home, get tips on parenting, find out about the latest baby products, get information on health concerns, or search for toys, you will enjoy exploring these sites.

Baby Center
Information, support, and products for pregnancy, baby, and toddler.
http://www.babycenter.com

Dr. Toy's Guide on the Internet
Information on hundreds of recommended toys and products for children
htttp://wwww.drtoy.com

Family
The parenting e-zine from Disney
http://www.family.go.com

Family Education Network
Advice for parents on how to help children learn
http://www.familyeducation.com/home

Kids Doctor Searchable Database of Pediatric Advice
Information on children's health issues
http://www.kidsdoctor.com

Resources *(cont.)*

Web Sites *(cont.)*

Kids Health Organization
Articles on Children's Health
http://www.kidhealth.org/index2.html

Kidsource
Online information for parents on child health, education, and more
http://www.kidsource.com

Pampers Parenting Institute
Information on infant and toddler care
http://www.pampers.com/index.html

Parents as Teachers National Center
Information to increase parents' awareness of young children's development
http://www.patnc.org/home.html

Parent Soup
This site includes parenting tips, discussions, and a baby name finder
http://www.parentsoup.com

Parent Time
A parenting e-zine from *Time Magazine*.
http://www.parenttime.com

Zero to Three
Lots of information on infants and toddlers for both parents and professionals
http://www.zerotothree.org